I AM VALUABLE

ADRIANE M. WOODS

Copyright © Adriane Woods Ministries, 2022. All rights reserved.

No part of this publication may be reproduced, redistributed, taught, stored in a retrieval system, or transmitted, in any form or by any means, electronic, mechanical, photocopy, recording, or otherwise, without the prior written permission of the publisher

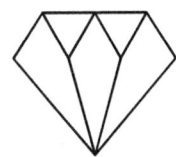

TABLE OF CONTENTS

ACKNOWLEDGEMENTS	5
INTRODUCTION	7
CHAPTER 1 THE WOMAN	19
CHAPTER 2 VASHTI	27
CHAPTER 3 THE DIAMOND	31
CHAPTER 4 THE CUT	39
CHAPTER 5 THE COLOR	51
CHAPTER 6 THE CARAT	65
CHAPTER 7 THE CLARITY	77
CHAPTER 8 THE PRESSURE	85
CHAPTER 9 THE RESOLUTION	93
CONCLUSION	101

This book is dedicated to:

My Grandmother, Luella W. Mack

&

My Mother, Mary Mack

ACKNOWLEDGEMENTS

I thank God for the inspiration and grace to finish this work.

To my husband Sterling R. Woods, Sr., I love and appreciate you. Thank you for your unconditional love and support of all of me and all that I do. I am forever grateful for US.

To my children, Asa, Ashton, Sterling Jr, Victoria, and Nadia, you are each a precious gift from God. I love you. Thank you for pushing me to pursue my dreams and live out my purpose.

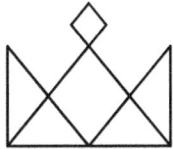

INTRODUCTION

"A woman of faith knows success is found in trusting God to counsel and guide the best pathway for her life."

—**April Williams**

I remember my grandmother once told me: *"If you accept who they say you are, then they never have to accept and respect you for who you really are."*

Luella Mack, my grandmother, and my grandfather, Rev. George Mack Jr, raised me as though I were their own. There were many great memories and nuggets of knowledge they shared with me; however, this is the one that helped shape my life and future in more ways than I was willing to acknowledge at the time. I was a child when this was spoken to me, and quite frankly, it was the last thing I wanted to hear. There was an event happening that I wanted to attend, and that quote was what she spoke to me amid telling me "**NO**," I could not attend. I can remember being so upset with her at that moment; I cried myself to sleep, all the while thinking to myself, why is she so mean and why doesn't she understand? I am grateful that I lived long enough to come to an understanding of what she meant; but even more grateful that God allowed her to live long enough, that I was able to share with her the understanding gained and appreciate her for the strength she modeled, in standing firm in her convictions.

Growing in understanding, I learned that the infamous "they" will always be a factor in our lives, but it is up to us to determine just how "they" will be factored in. The world around us will always offer its opinion in an attempt to define who and what we are.

Can you remember growing up and uttering these words at one time or another on the playground? *"Sticks and stones may break my bones, but words can never hurt me!"* You've most likely heard this one as well: "I'm like rubber and you are like glue, anything you say bounces off of me and sticks on to you."

I don't know about you, but I remember using those words a time or two. Oh, the joy of youthful innocence. However, if we were totally honest, we would have to admit that some of those things that were said about us stuck. Not only did they stick, but we also internalized them, and they became part of the foundational premise for how we would view ourselves and others. Sometimes it has been used as a catalyst to achieve certain goals (like the times we work extra hard to accomplish a goal, "only because they said you never could"). Then there is the instance where it has become a clutch and a barrier (i.e., there is no need for me to try because they already told me I would fail regardless).

Often, the "they factor" is so subtle that we don't even realize just how much "they" have impacted our lives. It all comes down to what we value in this life. Permit me to ask, *"What do you value?"*

In Matthew 6:21, Jesus says, *"For where your treasure is, there your heart will be also."* What we treasure is what we value. Whatever that is for you, know that it will come to play a huge role in determining how you live.

The word 'value' is simply defined as relative worth, merit, or importance. We can attribute value to anything in life: It could be something Godly or ungodly. It's essential that we choose to value the things that God would hold in high esteem. When we treasure the things that will draw us nearer to God and help us to grow deeper in our faith, the very character of our hearts will expand in Godliness.

What I have learned in life is that there is a close-knit correlation between Honor and Value. It is impossible for to Honor what you do not Value.

But what does it mean to honor something or someone? To Honor, simply means to treat with high respect, great esteem. If you don't respect something or someone, you will never attribute true value to it or them.

In essence, it is impossible for you to Honor the gifts within you if you are unable to see the value of YOU. God has given each of us gifts that are unique to us. He knows us better than we know ourselves, and He has equipped us with talents and a unique perspective that would drive us forward in fulfilling the glorious purpose He has prepared for our lives. But you must start with valuing yourself. After all, if you don't value yourself, how can you honor the gifts that the Lord has placed within you? If you don't honor those gifts, you will never develop them, put them into practice, or see through the divine purpose God has prepared for your life.

All of that becomes sounding brass if you don't understand just how valuable you are to God. How He has anointed and appointed the gift in you for such a time as this, to be a blessing to His Kingdom, but you still haven't committed to your yes.

In committing to your yes, you understand that God has already dressed you in purpose and prepared a divine purpose for your life. He has crafted you inside and out to be able to grow in and fulfill your purpose. It means that you believe that everything you need is already within you.

Just look at the beauty in His words in Psalm 139:13-14: "*For you created my inmost being; you knit me together in my mother's womb. I praise you because I am fearfully and wonderfully made; your works are wonderful; I know that full well.*"

God envisioned you before you were even born. He made every part of you, and He did so according to His glorious design. Saying yes to God is all about honoring the vision that God had when He made you. It's all about committing to developing and putting into action the unique giftings that God has put upon your life for the furtherance of the Kingdom of God. God made you a wonderful, unique woman with a purpose, and it's time for you to walk empowered in that truth.

Saying yes to God today solidifies your truth. God loves you more than you could ever know. Not only that, but His love is unconditional. Nothing can ever separate you from the love of God. Romans 8:38-39 says, "*For I am convinced that neither death nor life, neither angels nor demons, neither the present nor the future, nor any powers, neither height nor depth, nor anything else in all creation, will be able to separate us from the love of God that is in Christ Jesus our Lord."* No matter what you ever go through in life, God and His love will be there for you. You are precious, valuable, and irreplaceable to Him. If God Himself sees you this way, why is it so hard to look at yourself in the same manner?

Stop tearing yourself down. End any negative talk that you harbor against yourself. Denounce every curse ever spoken over you be it by others or self-inflicted; they have no place in your life anymore. Don't listen anymore to what anyone else says that you are: Instead, listen to who God says you are. Let Him define your identity and embrace that identity with all your heart.

Let's look at our best example, the Lord Jesus himself.

In Matthew 16:13-16, we see a discussion between Jesus and His disciples regarding the "they" factor:

"When Jesus came to the region of Caesarea Philippi, he asked his disciples, "Who do people say the Son of Man is?" They replied, "Some say John the Baptist; others say Elijah; and still others, Jeremiah or one of the prophets." "But what about you?" he asked. "Who do you say I am?" Simon Peter answered, "You are the Messiah, the Son of the living God.""

Jesus was aware that people who "knew of" him were talking about him, but He chose to focus on the opinion of those who "knew" Him, those who had spent intimate time with Him and understood His character.

It is one thing for others to have an opinion of you, but the guiding factor in how you live your life is really determined by how you see yourself. In the book of John, seven times Jesus uses the declaration "I Am" to describe Himself:

"And Jesus said to them, 'I am the bread of life. He who comes to Me shall never hunger, and he who believes in Me shall never thirst.'" -John 6:35

In this "I am" statement, Jesus uses symbolism that would resonate loudly within the hearts of his audience. The bread was a staple of most people's diets in those times (as it is for many of us today!) and it also holds significance in the Jewish people's place of worship, Solomon's temple in Jerusalem.

In the book of Exodus, while detailing how the tabernacle should be set up, God commands that bread shall be placed on a table in the tabernacle, continually. This bread would symbolize God's provision for the people. The bread would serve as a continual reminder that God provides for all our needs. After all, our most basic physical need is to eat, isn't it?

So, through this "I am" statement, Jesus is declaring Himself as the one through who we find sustenance and life. He will provide for all our needs: We will never hunger, and we will never thirst when we walk with Him. That truth applies to both our physical and spiritual lives. Jesus will never leave us lacking for anything.

Then Jesus spoke to them again, saying, *"I am the light of the world. He who follows Me shall not walk in darkness but have the light of life."* -John 8:12

This "I am" statement also carries with it incredible significance and imagery. Look at Genesis 1:1-3: *"In the beginning God created the heavens and the earth. Now the earth was formless and empty, darkness was over the surface of the deep, and the Spirit of God was hovering over the waters. And God said, "Let there be light," and there was light."*

In the beginning, the very first thing that God does as He begins the divine work of creation is to imbue the world with light. This light symbolizes godliness, holiness, and love. God's light is everything that makes God the perfect and loving God that we know Him to be.

There is still much darkness in the world today. No matter how close we are to God, because of our fallen nature, that darkness still taints our hearts. But through Jesus' sacrificial work of redemption on the cross, God's light will enter our hearts and banish the darkness. In Him, we find healing, forgiveness, and restoration from our sins.

Jesus is the very light of God, shining in a world that desperately needs His healing touch!

"<u>I am the door</u>. If anyone enters by Me, he will be saved, and will go in and out and find pasture." -John 10:9

When thinking of doors, we often use this imagery of speaking to opportunities in life. When an opportunity ends in life, we say that door has closed. When a new opportunity arises, we say a new door has opened. This "I am" statement captures that same idea but in a much bigger way. Jesus opens a door that no one else could open.

As a result of our fallen nature, our hearts are irrevocably tainted by sin. Because of this sin, we are separated from God in a way that we could never overcome. We are helpless on our own. Our hearts are too bound to the chains of sin.

Thank God for Jesus! He breaks the chains that bind our hearts and gives us freedom. John 8:36 says, *"If the Son has set you free, you are free indeed!"* That means you never have to return to the chains that once bound you. Jesus is waiting with open arms to lead you through the door that leads to salvation and eternal life.

"<u>I am the good shepherd</u>. *The good shepherd gives His life for the sheep.*" -John 10:11

A shepherd was a very common vocation in the life of those in Jesus' time. Even if it wasn't their personal job, it was a role with which everyone who heard Jesus' message would be familiar.

A shepherd devoted everything to his flock. Sheep on their own are vulnerable and easy prey. A shepherd would protect them from the dangers of the world at all costs, even up to their own life. A shepherd formed a bond with his sheep that could not be easily broken! He led them to safety and provided for all their needs.

We, like sheep, are subject to the many pitfalls and dangers of the world. We cannot make it through life safely, on our own! We need a shepherd to guide us, leading us into all holiness, righteousness, and love. Jesus is that shepherd, the One who gave up His very life to bring us salvation.

Jesus said to her, "<u>I am the resurrection and the life</u>. *He who believes in Me, though he may die, he shall live. And whoever lives and believes in Me shall never die. Do you believe this?*" -John 11:25, 26

God has given us many promises through His Word, but the greatest of all is the promise of eternal life. Why is that? Because sin and death are our ultimate enemies. Death feels like an inevitable end that we all must face. There's nothing we can do to escape it on our own.

But God's power is mightier than anything we will ever face, even sin and death itself! Jesus looked sin and death in the face, took on its full might, and then denied its power over Him. After three days in the grave, Jesus got back up and defied death!

In doing so, He won the ultimate victory over sin and death for us all. We no longer have to fear death because through Jesus we have eternal life. We, too, will rise again into our eternal life in God's glorious and everlasting Kingdom.

Jesus said to him, "*I am the way, the truth, and the life*. No one comes to the Father except through Me." -John 14:6

We are all looking for direction in life. Every one of us desires to make the next step in life toward the fulfillment of our purpose and destiny. That's why we buy so many self-help books, watch so many inspiring videos, and invest in anything we can that we believe will drive us forward in life.

This can get complicated and messy quickly. It's exactly why so many people end up looking for their purpose and identity in all the wrong places. This only leads them directly into a life of sin! But what if it was a lot simpler than we make it out to be? What if there was a singular way we all must go that would lead us each to our unique destiny?

That's exactly what the truth is. Jesus is the way that leads us to the ultimate truth of ourselves and the world in which we live. That truth leads us to eternal life in Jesus. In that eternal life, we will live forever by the side of our Father in heaven who loves us more than we could ever comprehend.

"*<u>I am the vine</u>; you are the branches. He who abides in Me, and I in him, bears much fruit; for without Me you can do nothing.*" -John 15:5

Consider the imagery of a vine for a moment. A vine bears fruit. It nourishes that fruit and provides it with everything it needs to bloom. As long as the fruit stays attached to the vine, it continues to thrive and produce more fruit.

Jesus fits this image perfectly in our world. When we are attached to Him, we continue to bear godly fruit in our lives. He provides the nourishment we need to bloom into everything God has created us to become.

Each "I Am" is followed by a confirming proclamation of who HE knows Himself to be. Jesus is firmly entrenched in His identity, and He is ready to share it with the world.

If I may ask you at this junction; do you know who you are? Now, how do you silence external voices if you don't know yourself? Your value is tied to your knowledge of yourself and your knowledge of yourself is tied to your knowledge of Christ. Our true identity is found in Him. Remember, no matter how valuable a product is; it'll be useless in your hand if you don't know what it's meant for. God created us for specific and unique purposes, but we don't realize how valuable we are and as a result, we underperform in virtually every area of our lives.

This book will unveil deep truths about the value of women both in God's kingdom and in the society at large. The woman God created in Genesis 1, 2, and 3 was given a specific assignment. Hence, we'll look at "The Woman" in the light of God's word. We shall highlight the general perspective of "what" women are and narrow it down to who you are as a woman. We are going to center our discussion around the story of Vashti from the book of Ester, a woman with a story that shows us the power that the spoken word can have in our lives. There is much more to her story than meets the eye, and we are going to plumb the depths of it to find what God is saying to us through it.

Do you know how much you mean to God? Do you know how much He loves and cares about you? I know it can be hard sometimes to navigate through all of the negativity "they" have spoken to you, about you, and over your life. However, my prayer is, by the time you finish this book, if someone were to ask you who are you, none of what "they" may have said or done will matter, because your response will at least start with: "I Am Valuable."

How then do I discover myself in the light of "My Value?" This book takes you on a journey of the "Making of Diamonds" in relation to how valuable we are as women.

I encourage you to stop intermittently and pray; as the Holy Spirit deals with you, journaling every step of the way, remembering, and recalling all that God will speak to you about through this journey of healing. Enjoy this book to the fullest!

CHAPTER 1
THE WOMAN

We will never be happy until we make God the source of our fulfilment and the answer to our longings. He is the only one who should have power over our souls.

--Stormie Omartian

We live in a world where sense of fulfilment is often tied to goals and achievements. However, when expectations are not met, depression, disappointment, and a sense of unfulfillment sets in. Women are prone to having more emotional breakdowns than men because according to God's original design, we are wired to be more emotional beings. As we live in a world that expects us to achieve certain goals at a certain age or time frame, we grow in the consciousness of linking our fulfilment to goals.

When we begin to live in the perspective of the world, we often forget that God is bigger than our limited human perspective and that through trust and faith in Him, we can accept that truth.

He knows the beginning from the end; thus, it is important to trust His infinite wisdom to guide your path.

You see, when God said, let us make man, he specified that man would be made in his image and likeness. Not only that, but man was also positioned for fruitfulness. Let's look together at Genesis: 1:26-30, "*Then God said, "Let us make mankind in our image, in our likeness, so that they may rule over the fish in the sea and the birds in the sky, over the livestock and all the wild animals, and over all the creatures that move along the ground." So, God created mankind in his own image, in the image of God he created them; male and female he created them. God blessed them and said to them, "Be fruitful and increase in number; fill the earth and subdue it. Rule over the fish in the sea and the birds in the sky and over every living creature that moves on the ground."*

Dear woman, God has created you in his image and has positioned you to be fruitful, productive, to have dominion and rule! In verse 26, when God creates humanity, it says that "*God created mankind in His image, male and female He created them.*" At first, it may seem as if this verse is simply repetitive, but there is much more going on here. There's a reason for the repetition.

Notice how both statements are slightly different. First, it simply says that God made mankind in His image. But then, the Bible makes sure that the reader understands a crucial truth: Male AND female was made in God's image. That means that the nature of a woman reflects something unique about the nature of God! Let this truth empower your identity as a woman. You are not just an ordinary woman, you have power, dominion and you have been positioned for productivity, increase, and to RULE because you have God's nature flowing in your veins. When we embrace this truth, it draws us ever closer to Him.

Genesis 2: 22-24 gives us a more intimate look at God's Creation of the female specifically:

And <u>Adam gave names</u> to all <u>cattle,</u> and to the <u>fowl</u> of the <u>air,</u> and to every <u>beast</u> of the <u>field;</u> but for <u>Adam</u> there was not <u>found</u> a help <u>meet</u> for him. And the <u>LORD God caused</u> a deep <u>sleep</u> to <u>fall</u> upon <u>Adam,</u> an d he <u>slept</u>: and he <u>took one</u> of his <u>ribs,</u> and closed <u>up</u> the <u>flesh</u> instead thereof; Then the LORD God made a woman from the rib he had taken out of the man, and he brought her to the man. The man said, "This is now bone of my bones and flesh of my flesh; she shall be called 'woman,' for she was taken out of man." That is why a man leaves his father and mother and is united with his wife, and they become one flesh.

This verse further shows the truth we uncovered in Genesis 1. God created both sexes unique, yet, reflecting His character and nature in some same but very different ways. Then, when they come together as one flesh in the sacrament of marriage, what happens? They reflect an even more profound example of God's life, love, and character to the world.

A wonderful example of this is how through the unity and love experienced in marriage, God grants us the ability to do what only He could previously do - Bring forth new life. This is just one of the many beautiful and remarkable ways that we reflect God's power, love, and character through the image He has placed within us.

Now, it's time that we explore how identity fuels our purpose. Genesis 3:20 says, "*And <u>Adam called</u> his <u>wife's name Eve;</u> because she was the <u>mother</u> of all <u>living.</u>"*

Adam was able to name every living thing God created; however, until Genesis 3, the female was only referred to as the woman, or the wife, whereby she had "labels." It wasn't until after the fall that her purpose was fully understood, and she would then be named Eve.

How we understand our identity will ultimately determine how our purpose plays out in our life. When Eve received her purpose, she also received her name. When we make our own "I am" statements, we piece together our identity as well.

For example, when you declare, "I am a daughter of God," you fuel that identity within yourself. This leads to you investing richly in Bible study, prayer, and fellowship, all things which will further your faith. You will begin to walk more intimately with the Holy Spirit in your life.

Another example would be to declare, "I am a person who is devoted to my physical health because God has given me stewardship over my body." This "I am" statement leads us to eat well, exercise, and live a healthier lifestyle. These are all things that honor God's gift to us of our physical selves and further prepare us for the purpose He has prepared for us.

But this truth also rings true on the other end of the spectrum. Proverbs 18:21 says, *"Death and life are in the power of the tongue: and they that love it shall eat the fruit thereof."* While our "I am" statements and positive declarations can produce life-giving fruit in our lives, so too can negative declarations bring out dangerous consequences in our lives.

When we look at Eve in the garden -- while she was deceived by the enemy -- it was her words spoken to Adam that ultimately gave birth to sin. We, too, are subject to this pitfall within our own lives. When we devalue ourselves, we don't bring honor to the design that God used when creating us. That leads us to stray further and further away from the purpose that God has prepared for us.

On the contrary, look how powerful our words of life can be! For Mary, it was her words of surrender that ultimately positioned her to give birth to the one (Jesus) who would set us free from the burden of sin.

Imagine the struggle the news brought by God's messenger would be on any one of us. She was told that she would conceive a child through the Holy Spirit and that He would be God's chosen one! That's a lot of pressure for anyone to shoulder!

But Mary trusts in the Lord through faith. She embraces this purpose and identity in her life through her response to God's messenger: *"Behold the handmaid of the Lord; be it unto me according to thy word."* This declaration of her identity in the Lord led her to faithfully live out her purpose as the mother of the Messiah Himself, Jesus Christ.

Let's look at one more example of the power of the spoken word that God has blessed women with throughout His story. Fast forward to Jesus' resurrection. His first encounter was with two women whom He instructed: "Go get my disciples and Peter." Through their obedience and their spoken word, others came to know that Jesus was not dead, He had risen from the grave! God used the power of the spoken word through them to bring life and value into the lives of others.

God never intended for His magnificent creation of the woman to be a silent and dormant creation. In fact, it was His master creation. He gave her life so that she could bring life, for without her it is impossible, and as such, she should never underestimate her value nor allow anyone else to.

You must know how purposeful God was when He created you. He didn't just make man in His image, but woman as well. He created THEM. He gave THEM dominion. He told THEM to be fruitful and multiply. You were given identity, you were given purpose, and you were given value at the very beginning. You are not less-than in any way and that was never God's intention when He created you. The Scriptures make that very clear. Are you willing to work in your God given purpose? I would like you to ponder on that.

In Genesis 2, God saw that there was no SUITABLE helpmate for Adam so, He created Eve from Adam. Eve had a divine purpose and that was to be a 'helpmate.' She was to be the mother of all human beings - No one could come into the world without her. So as God prepared to bring His only begotten Son into the world for our salvation, He did so through a woman!

Eve is never given her due in history. She is often criticized for her mistake but unrecognized for her essential role in the story of God's people. We all make mistakes: that's why there is grace and forgiveness in Christ. But none of us have the remarkable special role that Eve has fulfilled. She is the mother of all and God's chosen vessel through whom all humanity would derive.

In the original Hebrew, the name "Eve" is *Chavvah*. This is a word that carries significant meaning. The root of the word is *Chaya*, which means living, and the word *Chai*, which means life. The word *Chavvah* itself is in the causative form. This is because Eve caused everyone after her to live. She is the life-giver and mother of all, hence why Genesis 3:20 says, "*The man called his wife's name Chavvah, because she had become the mother of all the living.*"

Eve never let her mistake hold her back. She accepted God's judgment and carried on through life, still following Him. When she had children, she praised God for the miracle of childbirth. She walked through life alongside Adam just as God had ordained. She was faithful and true to the Lord throughout her life, and by God's grace, laid the building blocks of the human race.

Like Eve, we should be wise not to let our mistakes derail our mission in life. Sometimes, we get so distracted and discouraged by what we do wrong that we cease doing what we know is right. But that only perpetuates more sin in our lives. We must embrace God's forgiveness and step forward boldly in whatever it is that God has called us to do in life. In doing so, we will live a life pleasing to Him. We need to accept, embrace, and walk in our divine purpose as daughters of the Lord.

You need to scream this from the rooftops: I'm going to be who God has called me to be! I'm going to live in my purpose!

Your declaration of this purpose will be your first and most important step in accomplishing it. You must envision it and believe that you can do it before you can make it happen. Reflect on God's creation of you. Reflect upon God's creation of the woman. Remember everything that God has called you to be. You got this!

You are not alone! God has called you to fulfil purpose and He will put many upon your path to help encourage, guide, and support you along the way. Invest richly in these relationships and never let pride get in the way of accepting Godly help, wisdom, and guidance from others.

In the Gospel of Matthew, we find a genealogy of Jesus. Genealogies were important to the Jewish people. Through them, they were able to trace back their family lineage. This was crucial to them because they held a lot of honor and value in their family lines.

Being a patriarchal society, the genealogies typically only included men. But Jesus' genealogy is unique, as it contains four women: Tamar, Rahab, Ruth, and Bathsheba. Not only is it strange at first glance that these women are included, but even more curious when you realize these are all women who were known to have questionable reputations.

Why then would Matthew include these four women in the genealogy of Jesus? Each of these women had value despite their labels or lives. They each have undeniable significance to the birth of Christ. Each woman had a role to play in the story of God's people that ultimately led to the birth of the Messiah through the line of David, as it was prophesied.

Each made mistakes, as we all do. But despite those mistakes, they all ended up embracing their identity and purpose in the Lord. Every one of these women had a purpose that played a role in moving history along toward the prophesied birth of Jesus.

They are all prime examples of how valuing ourselves, despite our flaws and mistakes, can lead us to purpose beyond our wildest dreams! God has created us to be powerful and to make an impact in this world for the glory of His Kingdom. Are you ready to step forward in your divinely orchestrated purpose today?

CHAPTER 2
VASHTI

"If we are to better the future, we must disturb the present."

- Catherine Booth

When reading the book of Esther, Vashti is a character that is often sadly overlooked because we are typically focused on the character of Esther. But the inclusion of Vashti's story is important, and there is much we can learn from her character.

Vashti was the wife of King Xerxes (or Ahasuerus in many translations). Queen Vashti's story is set in about 480 BC in Susa, the capital of the Persian Empire which was ruled by Xerxes (485–464 BC). At that time, the Persian Empire was the largest the world had ever seen. It covered modern-day Turkey, Iraq, Iran, Pakistan, Jordan, Lebanon, and Israel, as well as parts of modern-day Egypt, Sudan, Libya, and Arabia.

History suggests that Xerxes' massive military campaign against the Greeks occurred between the events recorded in Esther Chapter 1 and 2. It's possible that Xerxes' feast in Esther 1 doubled as strategy sessions for the upcoming Greek campaign.

Esther 1: 10-12 reads:

On the seventh day, when King Xerxes was in high spirits from wine, he commanded the seven eunuchs who served him—Mehuman, Biztha, Harbona, Bigtha, Abagtha, Zethar and Karkas— to bring before him Queen Vashti, wearing her royal crown, in order to display her beauty to the people and nobles, for she was lovely to look at. But when the attendants delivered the king's command, Queen Vashti refused to come. Then the king became furious and burned with anger.

The verse above tells us that a great feast was held for the men of Susa. The city of Susa was founded sometime before the nation of Persia became prominent over the Babylonian Empire. By the time the Babylonian Empire had seized Jerusalem, the Persian Empire was already recognized as a rivaling nation.

The feast lasted for 187 days, during which time Vashti was busy hosting a party herself for the women. On the seventh day of the feast, King Xerxes commanded Queen Vashti to put on her royal crown and come to the men's party, so that he could parade her beauty in front of them (Esther 1:10–11).

Queen Vashti refused to come, igniting the anger of King Xerxes (verse 12). Even though he was attempting to bring disrespect to his wife, he still felt humiliated that she would disobey him in front of everyone at the party he was hosting. The king's advisors told him that he couldn't let her actions go unpunished, believing that other women would say, *"If Queen Vashti can get away with disrespecting her husband, so can I"* (verses 16–18).

King Xerxes sent out a royal edict stating the following: Queen Vashti was to be banished from the kingdom, and that he would give her position as queen to another woman worthier than she (Esther 1:19–21).

Vashti refused to be treated as less-than by her husband, even though it was unthinkable in those times and in her situation to say no. After all, her husband was the king, and what he said was law in that place and time. According to the society in which she lived; she didn't have many rights. We must remember this as we consider her story because it really drives home the impact of her disobedience.

She stood up to her husband, the King, at great personal cost. But in doing so, she spoke identity, purpose, and value into her life. She refused to have her value and worth, stepped upon. She knew the power her declaration would have, and she stood tall in it.

Living righteously doesn't always come easy. Sometimes, saying and doing the right thing can cost us. Remember, even Jesus Himself suffered! But doing the right thing ALWAYS brings us to a place of greater purpose, identity, and value in life. That's the remarkable lesson we learn from Vashti.

Just as Vashti spoke value into her life by not giving in to the King's demands, we too can speak out against those that would attempt to demean us in life as well. Resist the urge to be a people pleaser! If you have the tendency to say "yes" all the time to people, you must learn to resist that urge. Saying "yes" isn't always the right thing to do! There is an incredible power in saying "no" at the appropriate times.

Just consider Vashti's situation for a moment. A lot of people would have said "yes" to the king's demands for a multitude of reasons. First, he was the king, and his word was law. It was considered foolishness to disobey the king as severe consequences would come upon you for doing so. Secondly, not only was he the king, but also her husband. That was a time and place where a wife was expected to obey her husband at all costs. Not only that but her position as the queen was also at stake. While her choice was loaded with consequences, she still made the choice to uphold her dignity and worth no matter what the cost.

Most times, we make wrong decisions in a bid to satisfy the other party and not necessarily because we want to. Going forward, I want you to make a commitment to put the God perspective first in all you do. A good example is to ask yourself, "If Jesus were in my shoes, what would he have done?"

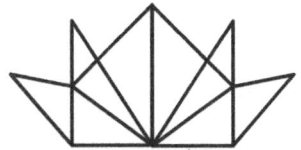

CHAPTER 3
THE DIAMOND

"No one can make you feel inferior without your consent."

-Eleanor Roosevelt

I am sure like me; you have heard the saying "A diamond is a girl's best friend." I never really understood why until I began to look at the creation of and various characteristics of a diamond. I realized how closely they align with the beauty of God's creation of a woman as we will discover along the journey in this book. The word 'diamond' comes from the Greek word Adamas which means "unbreakable." For foundational reference, let's look at the basics of how diamonds are formed and the characteristics of a diamond.

Diamonds were formed many years ago, deep within the Earth's crusts as intense pressure and temperature compressed ordinary carbon into the hardest crystals in nature. Then these stones were brought to the surface by cataclysmic volcanic activity. This explains why no two natural diamonds are alike. And why, it takes highly sophisticated mining methods and much time to extract rough diamonds. Very rarely were the conditions in which a diamond was formed completely devoid of other elements and those elements would get trapped in the carbon and become part of the diamond. This is how diamonds not only get inclusions (tiny particles of debris trapped in the stone) but also how they get their color. In addition, the diamond must go through many phases from the mining of the rough diamond to becoming the polished final product that we are accustomed to seeing.

There is a standard of classification of diamonds with regards to their certification. Diamonds are graded on a scale of 0-10 (with Zero (0) being the highest quality rating), and it is all subdivided into four distinctive categories, Cut, Color, Clarity, and Carat, also known in the industry as the 4Cs.

The Diamond's Cut

Of all the 4Cs, the cut has the greatest effect on a diamond's beauty. In determining the quality of the cut, the grader evaluates the cutter's skill in the fashioning of the diamond. The more precise the cut, the more captivating the diamond is to the naked eye. While the cut of a diamond may seem to indicate its shape, instead, what it refers to is its proportion, symmetry, and polish. The cut of the diamond is an irreplaceable factor that determines its overall beauty.

The beauty of a diamond is not in its raw state rather, it lies in the polished final product. God has 'cut' us into perfection and he awaits us to unlock every potential he has given unto us.

In the book of Jeremiah, God asked Prophet Jeremiah to visit the potter's shop.

Jeremiah 18:3-4 says, *"So I did as he told me and found the potter working on his wheel. But the jar he was making did not turn out as he had hoped, so he crushed it into a lump of clay and started over again."*

God has fashioned you uniquely and there is no one else in the world that is like you. You are a perfect cut from God, and you shine brilliantly in your uniqueness.

When you look at a high-quality diamond, you will see flashes of color deep within the stone, glinting sparks of red, orange, yellow, green, blue, and purple as light ricochets over the cut facets. To achieve that effect, diamond cutters must utilize the full effect of their skills. They must create precise cuts with immense skill. If they don't, they won't capture the fullness of the brilliance within the white light and the diamond will never show off its full potential.

Stop holding back your shine, you are a rare diamond. Allow the world to bask in the brilliance God has placed in you.

The Color

Diamonds are completely clear, aren't they? Not quite! Diamonds contain subtle colors within them. When rating diamonds, color is looked at more in terms of rarity. Completely colorless diamonds are the rarest, which makes them the most valuable!

Diamonds come from the ground, meaning they can typically contain yellow, brown, or gray colors because of things they pick up on the earth. For color variations in diamonds, it's typically due to other trace elements being present during its formation that give their color. How much of that element was present determines how many hues the diamond will have, and subsequently, how much it's worth!

Beloved, environment matters even to diamonds. Now the question boils down to what you permit to reflect in your life from your environment. Naomi had two daughter-in- laws, however, only Ruth stayed with her after the death of her husband and sons. Ruth's character reflected a woman with strong conviction and principles, one doused with humility and determination.

Ruth boldly declared to Naomi, "*Wherever you die, I will die, and there I will be buried. May the Lord punish me severely if I allow anything but death to separate us!*" (Ruth 1:17-18)

From the text above we can see that Ruth was a diamond that reflected genuine love for her mother-in-law. Her sacrifice paid off as through her came the lineage of David and Christ Jesus.

Clarity

Diamond clarity is the assessment of small imperfections on the surface and within the stone. Surface flaws are called blemishes, while internal defects are known as inclusions. In most cases, a diamond's beauty is not affected by inclusions since they can't be seen with the naked eye.

The clarity of a diamond is determined by its purity and rarity. Gemologists have a numeric scale that they use when making these determinations. The fewer imperfections and flaws in a diamond's appearance, the higher the clarity grade. No diamond is perfectly clear and pure, but the closer it gets to purity, the clearer it becomes. The diamonds with the highest values are the ones that are graded the purest.

Remember, all diamonds are unique, not perfect. It is totally okay to be imperfect but what is not okay is allowing your imperfections take a toll over your life. Dear diamond, God has called us to walk in his perfection and not what we think perfection is. By modelling over lives in God's standard, we better understand how to walk in the clarity of his word and in the uniqueness which He has purposed for us.

When we walk with God's word and in the light of His word, he beams brightness in our imperfections and teaches us how to walk in his light. Before the coming of Jesus, law was prevalent, and one was judged by obedience or disobedience to the law. The Pharisees brought a woman caught in the act of adultery before Jesus and they referenced the Law of Moses which classified her punishment as death by stoning. Despite their accusation of her imperfection, this was what Jesus replied to them according to John 8:7-11, *"When they kept on questioning him, he straightened up and said to them, "Let any one of you who is without sin be the first to throw a stone at her." Again, he stooped down and wrote on the ground. At this, those who heard began to go away one at a time, the older ones first, until only Jesus was left, with the woman still standing there. Jesus straightened up and asked her, "Woman, where are they? Has no one condemned you?"*

Do not let your imperfections blind you of the unique purpose God has called you to function. Jesus' attitude tells us that He in no way expects or desires for us to be with blemish, but His expectation is that once we come into the truth of His word, that our heart will be firm enough to walk in the truth of His word and sin no more.

The Carat

The fourth and final C that is measured in the diamond's value is Carats. The carat is the diamond's physical weight that is measured in metric carats. Carat weight is the most objective of the 4Cs in that it is absolute; it involves no estimates, comparisons, or judgments.

The carat is the universally accepted measurement of a diamond. Carat (ct.) is a unit of weight measurement used exclusively for diamonds and gemstones. Carat is not the same thing as visual size, as carat measures weight, meaning that you can't see carat weight. Factors affecting carat weight in a diamond are density and shape.

Every diamond is unique and carries its own individual certification; however, regardless of the classification and/or certification, they all have value. And that is what I want each of you to understand, each of us are wonderfully and skillfully made by the master crafter, and like a diamond, we all have value. We are not made to be carbon copies, we do not have the same anointing, we do not all have the same spiritual gifts, but we all add value to the Kingdom of God.

You noticed that in the description of the 4C's of a diamond – Cut, Color, Clarity, and Carat, nowhere was the 5th C listed – Cubic Zirconia (or lab-created diamonds), and that is with purpose, because while to the naked eye, the Cubic Zirconia may have the appearance of a diamond, however, it has no quantitative value. What makes a natural diamond more valuable than a lab-grown diamond is the fact they are rare and finite. Over the last 35 years, natural diamonds have shown to appreciate in price by approximately 3% on average every year. The cost of lab-grown diamonds on the other hand continues to decline due to mass production. Only natural diamonds retain inherent value over time making them an investment and an heirloom.

Because you are a woman of God with true value, that is why like a natural diamond, you can weather the various storms of life, and yet you never look like what you have been through! Woman of God, know your worth! You are valuable! You are unique! You are one of a kind! You are more precious than and as rare as the rarest Gemstone!

There may be a lot of Cubic Zirconia's that come your way, but you must realize that while you are often imitated, you can never be duplicated!! Woman of God, you must know your worth! You are more precious and valuable than even the rarest and purest of diamonds. That's how the Lord sees you, and it's time that you start to look at yourself in the same way!

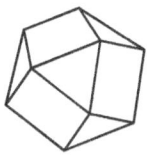

CHAPTER 4
THE CUT

"Imagine how differently you might approach each day by simply stating: God is good. God is good to me. God is good at being God. And today is yet another page in our great love story."

– Lysa TerKeurst

The cut is where the diamond's unique and beautiful characteristics start to come to life. The cut of the diamond determines how light will be reflected from and through it. Your life experiences and the way that you allow God to work through them determine your growth and how God's love reflects out of you and into the world. Remember Romans 8:28: *"We know that in all things God works for the good of those who love him, who have been called according to his purpose."*

Imagine for a moment Vashti's cut -- the hurt she must have felt when being summoned by the king to appear before him and his men wearing her crown. Vashti was at a crossroad, but she decisively refused to appear before the King. Like Vashti, many have experienced situations they thought would be the end of the road. Look at you today, your experiences have shaped who you are and who you are becoming, you are a living testimony of the goodness of God and his ability to bring anyone through what seems impossible. The master crafter, God Himself, allows things to happen to us in life only so that the best light within us can shine forth.

Of all the 4Cs, the cut has the greatest effect on a diamond's beauty. The light within reflects through the diamond according to the diamond's cut. In the same way, the cut, or the pain in your life, determines how light shines through you. When you process and walk through your pain in a godly way, God allows you to understand the situation from his perspective and even when you cannot fathom the situation, your unyielding trust in God assures you that He is in control.

No two diamonds are identical, making each a beautiful work of art. Diamonds are also tough (remember the word diamond means "unbreakable"). As humans we break down emotionally but by putting on God's armor, we wear the coat of resilience. This means that when others go through situations that would mar their lives, we go through the same seemingly dark and lonely road it's just that our path is neither lonely nor dark because we have God at the center of our lives. A real diamond can go through some things but still come out shining. A real diamond can cause some things to change, reflecting the light within in unique ways as it radiates it to the world. You are a diamond, and you embody all these things as well!

There's a reason why a woman can go through some stuff and come out of it not looking like what she's been through. Even when God told Eve after the sin that childbirth would be painful; God doesn't leave her without a promise and a blessing. The promise is once that child is in her arms, she doesn't even remember the pain of what she had just experienced because she is now face to face with her remarkable blessing from God.

What does this show us? That through God, our pain can bring beauty and purpose. It doesn't have to defeat us or keep us down. Following God's direction, we can use it as motivation to pull us back on our feet and propel us toward our divine purpose.

Your pain, your purpose, and God's unique plan for your life make you one of a kind, just like a diamond. God has fashioned you into the woman that you are just like a master jeweler creates his masterpiece.

Now that you know and embrace your value, it's time to walk in your worth. When you know who you are and what your purpose is in the Lord, you gain immeasurable power. You can then tear down every stronghold that the enemy places before you.

2 Corinthians 10:3-5 says:

> *For though we live in the world, we do not wage war as the world does. The weapons we fight with are not the weapons of the world. On the contrary, they have divine power to demolish strongholds. We demolish arguments and every pretension that sets itself up against the knowledge of God, and we take captive every thought to make it obedient to Christ.*

We must wield the power that God places within our hands. When we declare our identity and purpose, no schemes of evil can stand against us. We can speak words of empowerment into our hearts and be filled with everything we need to succeed in our

God-given purpose. As beautiful and powerful daughters of God, we can utilize our influence as image-bearers and make significant contributions to the world, all for the glory of God's Kingdom.

Living in God's purpose helps us to live in the consciousness of his standard and will. The popular story of the prodigal son (Luke 15:11-32) reflects the process of self-actualization - the point where he discovered servants in his father's house were leading a better life than he was. Just like the father of the prodigal son, God is always waiting for us with an open arm to welcome us home. Say, for instance, you've experienced pain that has made you feel less than or unimportant. Take those negative thoughts to the Lord in prayer and ask Him to cast away those troubling thoughts and replace them with ones of empowerment. He will help you to root yourself in your identity as His child.

Vashti's Cut

How did Vashti's cut influence her story? God used her pain for her purpose, just as He does in our lives. She has a lot to teach us about the cut and how we can come out shining on the other side. God used her in a mighty way to set His people free. I thank God for her and for her purpose.

Bible scholars will only tell you that she was defiant and disobedient. In doing so, they do Vashti a great injustice. She has a powerful voice, yet many will try to silence that voice. People are trying to silence your voice as well! People don't want to hear what you have to say. You are powerful in your identity in the Lord, and that kind of power intimidates people. But the Lord has called you to speak up and speak out, and He has put value in your words.

There will be times you will feel pressure to say "yes," even when you should say no. But look toward the example of Vashti. Vashti said no. No means no. We live in a time when people don't respect your no, but you must stand up for your value and worth, nonetheless. Don't let people silence your voice, even when they are putting pressure on you! They may try to make you feel less-than in the process, but don't fall for the deception. Cling tightly to your value.

Women are still looked at as sexual objects today. Just look at our story about Vashti. A party is going down, and it's a big one. The King of Persia is throwing a 187-day feast. The alcohol is flowing, and you can imagine things are getting out of hand.

Let that sink in for a moment: 187 days of straight partying! There was wine abound and it was plentiful. The king had invited everyone into the castle to have their fill. He spared no expense in making this the most lavish party imaginable. Everyone could drink as much as they desired and there was still plenty leftover.

During this elaborate and extended party, King Xerses hosted the men and Vashti hosted the women.

Now, you can bet that the king probably had his full share most of that 187-day period; and it is further proof that you can't make a sound decision in drunkenness. There's a reason why when you have a medical procedure done and you must be sedated, they make you sign something that says not to make any important decisions in the next 24-48 hours because they are giving you something that will alter your mind and decision-making process. Same thing applies to drunkenness, it alters your effective decision-making skills.

The king made a terrible decision in his drunkenness. He chose to disrespect his wife in what would have been one of the most humiliating ways possible. What he asked her to do was not a loving request in any way shape or form. It was not edifying to her or showing his devotion to their marriage.

On the contrary, it spits in the face of all these things. It was disrespectful to Vashti and their marriage. Instead of showing Vashti as his beloved wife and queen, he sought to objectify her like a trophy in his collection. His actions proved that he didn't care for her as his loving wife: She was just another one of his possessions. The king was rich, having so much that it blinded him from the irreplaceable gift that was his wife.

Sadly, many women throughout history have been subjected to such cruelty from the men who were supposed to love them. Marriage is supposed to be a relationship that builds us up and edifies us. Man and woman, both created in the image of God, are designed to come together in a way that only serves to reflect the image of God more brilliantly through them as a couple. They are designed to walk through life by each other's sides and striving in every way to serve one another in love.

Needless to say, this wasn't the experience that Vashti was having with Xerses. We're not sure how things were going up until this point: It's possible they had what seemed to be a great relationship. But the king decided to throw it all away with his act of disrespect and cruelty toward his wife.

Vashti was before all her girls when her presence was requested at the King's party. He had asked her to wear her crown because he wanted to show off before everyone else! Can you imagine the anguish? I can hear her saying "I thought he loved me. I thought he cared about me. I thought we were in this together." At that point, the realization must have set in for Vashti, that either way, no matter the option she chose, it represented an end to her reign as Queen. If she submitted to the king's request, once the party was over, and life went back to normal, she would never be viewed the same again by anyone in the kingdom male or female after exposing herself in such a demeaning manner in front of all the men of the kingdom. I can only imagine the internal reflection prior to making her decision having to answer the question posed to herself "Who Am I"? Am I the title? Am I the "stuff" that comes along with having the title? It is evident by her response and refusal to honor the request of the king that she determined that she was so much more; she chose her dignity, value, and self-worth. There are some times and moments in life where things will cut you, but you can still stand in faith knowing that God is with you.

Vashti held on to her right to say no. She held on to her worth. We would be wise to do the same. Many of us are unaware that our systems have been tampered with because of how we were treated in the past. No one deserves to be objectified or treated like they are less of a human being. If the terms of the relationship don't fit into God's standard, it is **TOTALLY OKAY TO SAY NO!** God has called you to be so much more, never let anyone define your standards or personality, live in the consciousness of your unique purpose.

The Beauty in Healing

Years ago, I had surgery on my back. Before the surgery. I was living bent over meaning I could barely take two steps without having to stop and recover. Some of you are living in your before the surgery. Some of you are living bent over – meaning you are not operating in your full potential; you have settled for less.

When God allowed the surgeon's hand to cut me, the surgeon said, "I don't even know how you were walking. Your nerve endings were so compressed that they were blue. You shouldn't have been able to walk at all."

I couldn't see beyond getting the surgery done and being able to walk in my pumps. You see, at that point I was confined within my limited knowledge and ideas, the joy of walking in some cute shoes again had been enough reason to bear the pain but something happened…

God spoke into my life and told me, *"Do you think you endured all that pain just to wear pumps? No. That pain was for your purpose. You can't walk in your purpose bent over and oppressed, telling others that God is a healer when you haven't been healed yourself. I needed to heal you so that when you speak about the healing of God; when you talk about what I can do in and through somebody's life, you can do it in conviction and say that if He can do it for me, He can do it for you! When the surgeon told you it was a miracle you were walking, that miracle I performed was for your purpose. Now people can know that God is a miracle worker and that when you say that you can do it with conviction!"*

I found it amazing that I would have to endure the worst pain in my life just to be able to live pain-free. When I think of it, it reminds me of a conversation between Jesus and the man at the gate when he asks, "Do you want to be made whole"? What I have come to understand is that I was "healed" when the 8-hour surgery was completed; in that the root cause of the issue had been resolved at the surgeon's hands. However, the process for me to become "whole" again and fully recover would take three months of intensive physical therapy (which started before I was even allowed to leave the hospital). I used to be of the mindset, "I can't fight for you and fight with you" – little did I realize I would be the person I was ultimately fighting both with and for. During the physical therapy, there were many days and nights when I cried myself to sleep in pain; unwilling to face the next day because all I could see was another day of pain ahead of me — it was not easy. I recall going to my follow-up appointment a week after my operation with a walker and moving at a turtle's pace. When the surgeon arrived, I wanted to talk to him about how much pain I was in, but he was more interested in how "beautiful the cuts were healing" (the surgery required me to have a 6-in cut in both the front and back). I was in pain and had a "slight" attitude, so I questioned, "If you are so good, why did a procedure that was meant to take three hours turn into over eight hours, and is that the reason I was in so much discomfort?" I am guessing he was accustomed to grumpy patients in pain just a few days out of major surgery, so my "slight attitude" did not faze him one bit. He went on to explain to me that when he began to remove the damaged disc from my back; they were so fragmented there were "pieces" along my nerves, and he had to take extra caution not to damage the nerves while removing the damaged particles. He went on to tell me "I know because of your pain, "today" you do not like me; but I promise you, when all is said and done, and you have fully recovered, you are going to love me." He wasn't arrogant; he was a man of God who understood that he was nothing more than a vessel. Countless times, I had an internal struggle doubting my perseverance due to the pain. I fought myself, every time I told myself "You can't do it, the agony is too great" or "this is good enough, you don't have to keep going, you can stop right here," it was a war - but today I can say I thank God for his grace in allowing me to persist. You have to realize that when it comes to your healing; many times, the greatest battle will be the internal battles you will have to fight to overcome; but know that you are worth it, and you are worth fighting for.

Let's look at it again from what we know about the cut of a diamond "*The cut of the diamond is an irreplaceable factor that determines its overall beauty. The better the cut, the stronger a diamond's ability to reflect light. Diamond cutters know the best cuts to make in order for the diamond to refract the most light.* Remember how I shared that the surgeon overlooked my pain and focused on how the "cuts" were healing. You see, as a surgeon and being a master at his craft, he understood that when the healing process was complete, and I was able to live pain-free, what would remain would be the visual results (scarring or lack thereof) from the way the cuts would heal and would always be there to remind me of what I had overcome. He knew when I looked upon it, it did not need to be something that would bring me yet another place of pain, but instead, it needed to be something that can be looked upon as beauty for my ashes and a reminder of what God had done in my life. My healing was so remarkable it even astonished the physicians. And yes, when I was finally released from the care of the surgeon, I confessed to him that what he shared about me "loving" him, once I was fully healed was accurate and that I did love him and appreciated him for putting up with my "slight attitude" and thanked him for allowing God to use him in my healing process.

Just think about it with me for a moment. If the surgeon can be so confident in the formation and beauty in the healing of the cuts through a surgical process; how much more confident do you think the master creator is in the thoughts that He thinks towards you? There is nothing in life that God will not accompany us through. We must decide whether or not we are worth fighting for and with.

In John 8:12 Jesus says, *"I am the light of the world. He who follows Me shall not walk in darkness but have the light of life."* God intends that we accept His light of Joy, Peace, and Hope, so that when we look back on our situations, we will no longer see the shadow of the dark place we were in, but rather the light of abundant life Christ has promised us. The brilliance of Christ's light will shine brightly in and through you. You are so very worth it woman of God. Don't be afraid to do the work that is necessary to get through to the brilliance of your cut.

While going through the intensive physical therapy sessions; the therapist shared with me that many people never fully recover nor get the expected results because they give up and don't follow through with the required sessions. While your healing may not take you to a physical therapist, it may be a counselor or another type of therapist; dear woman of God, do whatever it takes to bring you to a better place where you can live your life whole again. We serve a God that can take your pain, take your ashes, and turn them into beauty. You're still here, you still have a reason to praise God. After all you've been through, you can still have joy. After all that hurt, God can still bring you healing and deliverance. He is the God of healing and restoration, and He will work through your hurt in a mighty way! There is beauty in your healing!

CHAPTER 5
THE COLOR

"Now I know that the best thing I can offer to this world is not my force or energy, but a well-tended spirit, a wise and brave soul."

–Shauna Niequist

There are some things you've gone through in your life that the enemy is attempting to derail you with. What were you trained to do because of the times or setting in which you grew up in? Were you trained to keep your mouth shut? Were you taught that what happened in "the house" stayed in the house? Was your mind programmed for success of failure?

Often, the environment is overlooked however, it is a key factor that helps shape our thoughts and how we see the world at large. The color of a diamond is largely determined by where and when it was mined. So, if the outcome of a diamond is determined by its environment, how much more, you! Whatever situation you may be going through, it's time for you to have a voice, it's time for you to speak out. There's a woman out there waiting to hear your story of deliverance. You never know the impact that your story can have on the life of another! There's a woman out there who needs to know about the trials you went through and overcame because she's going through them herself and she feels alone. She needs to know that there's someone she can relate to, she needs to believe that God will reach into her life just as He did for you.

Vashti's denial was made more powerful by the setting and the times. A woman didn't say no back then, especially to her husband, and even more so if he was a king! There are so many layers of things going on in Vashti's story that makes her refusal even more shocking. Very few (if any) women would have done what she did in their era.

Women were rendered voiceless at the time and even now there are some people who do not believe a woman should have a voice. The King's fury at her disobedience wasn't only about Vashti; it was also about the many people who would follow her. He realized that her example would enflame the feelings of the other women in the kingdom, as well as cause them to question men's authority over women.

In a lot of ways, we are still living in what I call the shhhhh generation. Many people would like to silence your voice because they are afraid of your strength. However, you must not remain silent. It will determine your freedom and that of countless others who are tied to you.

The new Aladdin live-action adaptation from Disney was updated to include a powerful scene with Jasmine. Even though she is the Sultan's daughter, the villain Jafar is urgently trying to silence her. Despite Jafar's threats, she has something important to say and refuses to remain silent.

She sings a powerful song at that moment, entitled *Speechless*. She proudly exclaims how she won't silence her voice no matter what may come against her. And in the end, her words are powerful and bring her to lead her people as their first female Sultan.

When you take care of yourself, you can take care of everyone else. Philippians 4:13 says, "*I can do all things through Christ who strengthens me.*" To be able to do this, you must first be healed yourself. God has already given you everything you need to come out of your troubles stronger on the other side. All you have to do is agree! Remember the question Jesus asked the man at the pool of Bethsaida: Do you want to be healed? This is the question He asks you today. Make your answer a resounding YES!

Guard Your Heart

We can often be our own enemies as sin has become an essential part of the human experience. So much of what we face every day is an internal rather than external battle. When we don't test our ideas, feelings, and wants against God's perfect will, they often lead us astray. They lead us to begin conducting our lives according to the ways of the world rather than the ways of God's Word.

Proverbs 4:23 tells us to, "guard our heart." Guarding your heart suggests an attack or protection over a future attack because there will be things that try to distract you from God's purpose, plan, and goal for your life. Life is a spiritual battleground! The truth is that we live in a world that is overrun by distractions. The enemy will use every weapon at his disposal to try to pull you away from the important mission God has given you. He's terrified of you completing what God has called you to. As a result, we must defend our hearts against all his schemes and attacks.

Offense and bitterness are prime examples of areas that creep into our hearts and attack us from the inside out. We tend to be very self-defensive when facing conflict. The injustice that we have experienced, or think we've experienced, leads to us losing control of our better judgment. We stop seeking what is best for the other person and the relationship, instead choosing to hurl whatever hurtful words and actions are necessary to defend ourselves.

This type of attitude will hinder your peace, take your joy, and rob you of the faith needed to move mountains. When you live in this way, the enemy has won. You are falling right into his traps. We must be quick to recognize these tendencies and avoid them at all costs.

How do we guard our hearts? By investing deeply in God's Word, prayer, and fellowship. There are no replacements for the spiritual disciples in the life of a Christ-follower. The incomparable truth of the Bible reveals God's wisdom to us, reveals our purpose and helps us to understand God's character. Prayer is the way that we communicate with God, building our personal and intimate relationship with Him. Fellowship is where we find encouragement the likes of which we can find nowhere else.

God's Word gives us the wisdom and truth that help us to determine what is right from wrong. The truth of the matter is that sometimes there are things in life that may seem good, but in actuality are not. That's because Satan loves to disguise evil things as good to try to ensnare us in evil. Because of this, it can be quite challenging to recognize good from evil sometimes. That's precisely why a lot of people, even with good intentions, do a lot of evil in this world!

The Bible contains within its pages the very words of God, given to the biblical authors to write. His truth abounds on every page, giving to us profound wisdom, insight, and truth straight from the heart of God Himself. We must commit to a daily Bible-reading plan. It's vital that we dive deeply into the Scriptures and bind the wisdom we find there deep within our hearts. When we do, we will be ready when the moment strikes when we must discern good from evil in our daily lives. Our hearts and minds will be saturated in God's truth, and we'll know exactly what to do according to God's will.

Another important aspect of the Christian faith is prayer. If we are to fully live out what we learn in God's Word on a daily basis, we must have open lines of communication with Him throughout our lives! Every relationship requires communication, and prayer is how we communicate with God! Prayer is the means by which God instills in us and teaches us how to live out what we learn through His Word.

As our relationship with God grows deeper and deeper, so too does the barrier of strength that forms around our hearts.

The more we speak with Him, the more we realize His ultimate power, goodness, and love for us. We then have the assurance that He is continually fighting for us and will NEVER let us down. We know that we can trust in the strength He provides us, the strength to guard our hearts.

Fellowship is another aspect of our faith that we'd be foolish to ignore. God is a relational being Himself, and He created us in His image! So, that means we are to live rational lives as well. We were made to live out our lives in unison with our brothers and sisters in Christ. In these bonds we form with our family of faith, we find added strength and encouragement for our journey. Having others with the same beliefs alongside us will only serve to strengthen our convictions, knowledge of God's Word, and relationship with Him. When we engage in meaningful relationships with other believers, we experience Christ's presence in a whole new way! In Matthew 18:20, Jesus says, *"For where two or three are gathered in my name, there am I among them."* When the body of Christ comes together, He is right there with us!

Another aspect of fellowship that aids us so much in spiritual warfare is accountability. There is no replacing a sound accountability partner in the life of a Christian. This person must be someone in the faith, and someone that we know without a doubt that we can trust. Otherwise, it can be anyone!

What makes an accountability partner such a powerful ally in battling against the schemes of Satan? An accountability partner knows where we struggle with sin and joins up with us in our battle against it. They help us to set goals and standards that will define our battle against our sin. Then they regularly check in with us, making sure that we are sticking to the goals and standards we have set forth.

All of these things put together will help you to guard your heart. The more you invest your time and energy into the spiritual disciplines, the stronger and more resilient your heart will become against the schemes of the devil. These spiritual disciplines are all ways that we train ourselves in the faith to become stronger and stronger in our roles as children of God.

This is of utmost importance because the condition of our hearts determines the course of our lives. When our hearts are saturated in God's love, that love radiates outward and touches the lives of everyone we meet. When our hearts are drowned and held back by sin, that evil spews forth from within and causes destruction in its wake.

Guarding our hearts means living a life centered around God's truth. When you live in this way, God's love pours through you and creates an impenetrable barrier around your heart. God's truth and love will protect you from anything that ever comes against you. Fortify yourself in the Lord and guard your heart above all else.

We live in a world riddled with anxiety. People around us are hurting and seeking answers to their life's questions. Everyone appears to be going through a difficult time. Our ever-increasing responsibilities and schedules weigh us down. People yearn for peace, but it remains elusive. Something always seems to drag us away from taking the time we need to refocus and recenter.

The root of this cycle of fatigue and anxiety is uncertainty. We now have more technology and resources than ever before. It's difficult for us to admit that we don't have control. We want to be in charge of our own lives, but the truth is that we are not. We are terrified of coming to terms with this reality. We learn that no amount of bustle or effort can put us in control of our lives. However, this doesn't mean that we are without hope because we are daughters of God, and our Father is the ultimate architect of our lives. He longs to relieve us of the burden of trying to control things because we are in His hands. He wants to ease our hearts of the fear of uncertainty, so we can move forward and live lives of freedom and joy.

Romans 8:28 reads, "*We know that all things work together for good to those who love God, to those who are called according to His purpose.*" To break the death grip that uncertainty has on our hearts, we must remember that God makes everything work together for our good. If we put our trust in Him completely, we no longer have to deal with uncertainty. We can rest assured that our well-being is in the hands of the one and only God.

The recent pandemic is a prime example of the kind of uncertainty we experience in the world. People are facing losses on so many levels and all of which are infusing growing concerns in their lives. The pandemic is affecting everything both personal levels and worldwide levels: personal holistic health, families, jobs, finances, etc.

But God's power is still greater. This uncertainty we feel in these trying times is not a signal of the end. Humanity has faced innumerable trials, tragedies, and pandemics in the past. But God has pulled them through every single one. We must take this uncertainty and mold it into Faith: Faith that God loves us unconditionally and created us from an overflow of that love will deliver us from all evil and lead us on a path of eradicating all fear from our hearts. We must resist the urge to fall into fear and run into His loving arms instead.

Do Not Fear!

You will notice as you read your Bible that there are countless times throughout the Scriptures that when someone experiences God's presence in the form of a prophet, angel, or Jesus Himself, the first words that are spoken are, "Do not fear!"

The following story is from Mark 4:35-41:

That day when evening came, he said to his disciples, "Let us go over to the other side." Leaving the crowd behind, they took him along, just as he was, in the boat. There were also other boats with him. A furious squall came up, and the waves broke over the boat, so that it was nearly swamped. Jesus was in the stern, sleeping on a cushion. The disciples woke him and said to him, "Teacher, don't you care if we drown?" He got up, rebuked the wind, and said to the waves, "Quiet! Be still!" Then the wind died down and it was completely calm. He said to his disciples, "Why are you so afraid? Do you still have no faith?" They were terrified and asked each other, "Who is this? Even the wind and the waves obey him!"

In this story, we see Jesus' power and authority, even over the forces of nature!

Let's dig deeper into this story together. The disciples find themselves caught up in a violent storm on the water. Being in a strong storm on a boat is always a nerve-wracking experience, but this is even worse. The disciples are not on a sturdy, large, modern ship: they are in the shoddy boat of humble ancient fishermen. This boat is not designed to withstand the kind of punishment coming against it. Their very lives hang in the balance of riding out this storm.

There are many times when we are caught up in the violent storms of life. These storms come in a multitude of ways, and sometimes all at once. We may be facing physical illness, a loss of security, emotional distress, persecution, and so much more. As they say, when it rains, it storms. That's the place we all find ourselves in life at one point or the other.

And, just like the disciples, we too often doubt His power and influence over our lives. Just look at what the disciples did in this story. They did not trust in His power instead, they question Him, asking, "Don't you care if we drown?" They are pretty much saying, "What are you going to do about this?" That doesn't sound very trusting and reverent to me.

Why were the disciples acting in this manner? Because they were afraid. Fear has a funny way of making us act like someone else. Our natural response to fear is to try to protect ourselves at all costs, which can make us act irrationally. Sometimes fear is ok. For example, if you are walking across the street and a car is speeding by and you must quickly get out of the way when prompted by fear, then that's ok! Your life has been saved, that feeling will pass, and you'll go on with your life.

But oftentimes, we hold on to irrational fears. Fears such as finances, job security, relationships, etc. These are all things that we are told that God will provide, yet we still worry about them anyway. That is when fear is very unhealthy. This is the kind of fear that causes people to make rash decisions, destroys relationships, and creates a lot of unrest in people's hearts.

For evidence of this in this story, just look at the way the disciples treat Jesus all of a sudden! They throw accusations at him, asking if He cares that they might drown! Then, they make demands of Him, asking Him what He's going to do about their situation. That is all bursting forth from fear, a fear that has sprung forth because they were not trusting Jesus as they ought to be.

Back to the disciples on the boat. In the midst of their fear during the storm, Jesus asks them a profound and piercing question: Why are you afraid?

This is the same question that we must ask ourselves when we are enduring the trials of life. Why are we afraid? We know that Christ has already secured victory over sin and death, sharing that victory with us through faith. We know that His power and might are beyond anything that will ever come against us in life. What is it then that we have to be afraid of?

But, nonetheless, even though they doubt and lash out in fear, Jesus brings them salvation. And look at the ease with which He brings forth a solution! He merely commands the waves to be still, and nature itself obeys Him!

Imagine if you were in the disciples' shoes. At the point when Jesus starts talking to the storm, you're probably starting to wonder if this guy you've been following is actually just crazy after all. But then, the miraculous happens. The storm is calmed merely at the command of His words.

This turn of events was so shocking, so unparalleled, and so unlike anything they had ever witnessed before that the Bible tells us they were *terrified*. Put yourself in their shoes for a moment. I'm sure all of us have witnessed some pretty intense storms in our lives. Nature and the destruction it can bring can be downright frightening. It's so scary because we have no power over it. There's nothing we can do to stop a raging storm.

But Jesus stands there, and calmly does what no other is able to do. This display of might should bring immense comfort to our hearts. We must cling tightly to Jesus throughout every moment of our lives. Then, when the storms arise, as they inevitably will, Jesus will be right there to calm them with a single word.

We need His might in our lives to succeed in spiritual warfare, there's no doubt about it. That's why we must cultivate and cherish our relationship with Him now. The knowledge of His might fosters a deep trust in Him within us. That trust leads to an abounding peace that persists despite all circumstances. We start to understand that it doesn't matter what comes our way because the might of Jesus is on our side.

Healthy vs Unhealthy Fear

Proverbs 9:10 says, "*The fear of the* Lord *is the beginning of wisdom, And the knowledge of the Holy One is understanding.*" The fear of the Lord is something that is often misunderstood. We aren't to fear

God because He is malevolent, mean, or wishes us ill. God would never do us harm! He instead desires nothing more than to guide us, love us, and nurture us through life. Then what is all this talk in the Bible about "the fear of the Lord?" What are we to make of it?

Think back to when you were a child. You likely wished to please your parents. You had an innate "fear" of disappointing them, not because you thought they wouldn't love you if you did, but because you truly desired to follow their wishes for you. You love your parents, and you wanted to bring them joy! You had a reverence and respect for their authority in your life, and you didn't want to cross it.

God is our Father, and we are His children. We, too, must cultivate a healthy respect for His authority over us. That reverence for the Lord will guide us in all holiness. This is what **healthy fear** is all about!

This healthy fear of the Lord will help us defeat irrational fears in our life. How? By helping us to discern where our priorities should lie. For example, a healthy fear of the Lord helps us to understand that our focus must be set on the things of God, that which is eternal, instead of the things of the world, which are temporary. Instead of worrying about our everyday lives where God already has promised that He would provide, we must be focusing more on our eternal destiny and how we are preparing ourselves for the glorious day when it arrives.

Understanding a healthy fear of the Lord while casting aside unhealthy fear will help us to step into the fullness of our identity as women of God. It will also help us to understand how the experiences of our lives have led us to where we are today. We can trust in God to use them all for good.

CHAPTER 6
THE CARAT

"Just when we think we've messed up so badly that our lives are nothing but heaps of ashes, God pours His living water over us and mixes the ashes into clay. He then takes this clay and molds it into a vessel of beauty. After He fills us with His overflowing love, He can use us to pour His love into the hurting lives of others."

–Lysa TerKeurst

Carat weight is the most objective of the 4Cs in that it is absolute; it involves no estimates, comparisons, or judgments. God DID NOT make any mistakes when he created you, the Father's love for you is absolute and unconditional. He envisioned you and created you from an overflow of that love. You carry part of God within you, for you were made from His love. That truth alone fills you with value and worth as nothing else can.

It's beautiful and helpful to think of our relationship with God from a Father/daughter perspective. You know how precious little girls are to their daddies, and how attached those little girls are to their fathers. You've heard the term, "Daddy's girl" before. God desires to have a similar relationship with you. He adores you, and He wants you to cherish Him as well. He longs for you to come to Him with all of your needs so that He can take care of you the way that only He can. Be a "Daddy's girl" with your Father in heaven.

Cry out to your Father God in every circumstance you find yourself. You can rest assured that He will respond and help you and empower you every step along the way.

As you go through life, it's time to equip yourself with the full armor of God. God has given you each piece of this armor to protect you from the schemes and deceptions of the enemy. Ephesians 6:14-20 reads:

Stand therefore, having your loins girt about with truth, and having on the breastplate of righteousness; And your feet shod with the preparation of the gospel of peace; Above all, taking the shield of faith, wherewith ye shall be able to quench all the fiery darts of the wicked. And take the helmet of salvation, and the sword of the Spirit, which is the word of God: Praying always with all prayer and supplication in the Spirit, and watching thereunto with all perseverance and supplication for all saints; And for me, that utterance may be given unto me, that I may open my mouth boldly, to make known the mystery of the gospel, For which I am an ambassador in bonds: that therein I may speak boldly, as I ought to speak.

God has equipped you for a certain season, for a certain reason, and for a certain people. Daughter of God, it's time to use your voice to bring about powerful and profound manifestations of the Holy Spirit in your life.

What Happened to Vashti?

I began to ask the Lord, "What happened to Vashti?" All I could do was picture Vashti walking off alone in the sunset.

God's response about what happened to Vashti was simple. He responded, "She finished the race. Tell my daughters, you don't have to run this race by yourself." If you look at running at 1600, it's much more effective if you run it in a 4x4. It's not that you aren't capable of running the entire race alone, it's that you were designed to do it with assistance. The issue is we get so caught up in running, we don't look for assistance.

God has placed destiny helpers in your life. All you must do is trust in Him. Let's say you need the advice to sustain your marriage; You don't want to take advice from a single woman who has never been in your situation. You need someone who has been there, done that, someone who can tell you about all the nights they prayed for their husband, cried for their husband, and asked that God would come into their home; and honestly share with you what it takes. She can help you and encourage you on to the next leg of the race.

There are times when you can't take it on your own, times when you can't do the work by yourself. That's when you need to connect with a sister who can speak a word to you. Woman of God, you were not meant to run this race alone. God has so much for you, all you have to do is make the right connections. Invest richly into the relationships that will feed godly influence into your life.

He's going to give you the strength you need to finish the race and fulfill your purpose.

When you connect with women of God, they know how to pray for you like no one else can. They aren't out there talking about you, nor spreading your business, rather they are there praying for you powerful prayers of intercession. Sometimes when you can't pray for yourself, you need someone out there to intercede for you. James 5:16 reads, *"Therefore confess your sins to each other and pray for each other so that you may be healed. The prayer of a righteous person is powerful and effective."* God will undoubtedly use the prayers of others to bless your life in unimaginable ways.

Think back to the story of Job. There was a hedge of protection around him. Prayer puts a hedge of protection around you. The enemy can't do anything to you that God doesn't allow, and when He does, you don't have to be broken. Ask God, "What is your purpose in this? How can I come through this? God, help me through this?" The hedge is still there. The covering is still there. You are still protected, even in the midst of your pain.

You have the power of life and death in your tongue. YOUR BREAKTHROUGH IS WAITING FOR YOU! There are things you must expect by faith because you need to proclaim their existence before they even happen. You can take back everything the enemy has taken from you. In the name of Jesus, I'm coming to take my marriage back. In the name of Jesus, I'm coming to take my joy back. In the name of Jesus, I'm coming to take my hope back. In the name of Jesus, I'm coming to take my peace back.

Your breakthrough is understanding that no matter what you've been through, God has allowed things to happen in your life to birth a ministry in you to bring many to Him. Your pain had a purpose. Do you think God does it for sport? Absolutely not! When I went through the pain of surgery, I couldn't understand how I had to endure the worst pain of my life to live pain-free. Woman of God, work through all of the stuff because there is purpose on the other side of your healing. There is freedom on the other side of healing. There is hope on the other side of healing.

We cannot share our testimony until it is settled within us. There are so many people in this world who have not come to grips with vital parts of their story. What tends to happen is they stuff traumatic happenings or avoid painful memories only to come to the end of their lives bitter. If we are ever going to be people who help and equip others, we need to commit to doing the hard work of healing and accepting the story that has unfolded in our lives.

No matter where you are at in this journey, if you will do the hard work, Jesus is going to use it for His glory! You can stop running from the painful memories because the time is NOW to be all that God wants you to be. It is NEVER too late. Let's start claiming the scripture, *"I am not ashamed of the Gospel of Jesus Christ because it is His power in me!"* (Romans 1:16).

The Gospel is the story of Jesus, our Savior. Through the life that He lived, Jesus showed us firsthand the incredible power stories could have. His story changed the world as we know it, all the way up until today. His story brought the events of the world into fruition until this very day. If it wasn't for his story, you wouldn't be reading the book that is currently in your hands. Jesus, even though His appearance on Earth was over 2000 years ago, is still shaping your life through His story to this very day!

In Romans 1:16-18, Paul writes, *"For I am not ashamed of the gospel, because it is the power of God that brings salvation to everyone who believes: first to the Jew, then to the Gentile. For in the gospel the righteousness of God is revealed—a righteousness that is by faith from first to last, just as it is written: "The righteous will live by faith."*

The Gospel is the reason for our salvation. Without it, you wouldn't be able to experience the life-altering, profound relationship you have with God today. Our hearts should overflow with gratefulness because of what God has done through Jesus Christ. It is the most powerful testament to the power that our stories hold.

We must not be ashamed of our story. Our path has led us to where we are today. It doesn't matter who you are, where you've been, or what you've done: God will always welcome you into His open arms. His love for you is not inhibited by anything you've done, or that has happened in your life. His love is mightier than all.

Peter's Example

Peter is a prime example of someone who settles his sin and moves on in life to walk a path of freedom in the Lord. He was a fisherman who Jesus called to follow Him. But even during his time with Jesus, he is constantly doubting, messing up, and not living out his true potential. He is showing his human nature constantly and in every way. One profound example of this is the story of Jesus walking on water.

In this setting, the disciples find themselves on a boat in the middle of a terrifying storm. Now, to really let this story sink in, we must deeply consider their dire situation for a moment. They weren't on the water in a luxury boat of our times. They weren't even in the modest, humble boat of our times. They were in the most modest and humblest boats of ancient times. It had little to no defense against such brutal weather. Imagine the kind of boat a poor fisherman would own in those times. How do you think it would hold up in the face of a fierce and battering storm?

In this light, it's completely understandable why they would be terrified while trying to survive such a storm. The winds and waves battered their humble boat, and they must have felt as if it was just a matter of time until they would meet their watery demise. But Jesus was not only coming to save them. Jesus was coming to show them just what kind of legendary feats they were also capable of.

You've heard a million times about how Jesus walked on water. But do you ever hear people talking about how Peter walked on water as well? Matthew 14:28-29 reads, *"Lord, if it's you,"* Peter *replied, "tell me to come to you on the water." "Come," he said. Then Peter got down out of the boat, walked on the water, and came toward Jesus."* It's amazing that Jesus walked on water, yes, but we've come to see Him do many miraculous things. The essential part of this story is the fact that through the power of Jesus, Peter was able to do the miraculous as well!

Even though Peter was able to do something so amazing through Jesus, it still took some time for it to truly sink in and for Peter to grasp the full potential within him. This powerful moment for Peter happens after he spends time with the resurrected Jesus and Jesus forgives him for Peter's denying of Him in His time of trial. He then commissions Peter to continue His work on Earth and establish His church.

There's something else beautiful that happens here. John 21:15-17 reads:

> *When they had finished eating, Jesus said to Simon Peter, "Simon son of John, do you love me more than these?" "Yes, Lord," he said, "you know that I love you." Jesus said, "Feed my lambs." Again, Jesus said, "Simon son of John, do you love me?" He answered, "Yes, Lord, you know that I love you." Jesus said, "Take care of my sheep." The third time he said to him, "Simon son of John, do you love me?" Peter was hurt because Jesus asked him the third time, "Do you love me?" He said, "Lord, you know all things; you know that I love you." Jesus said, "Feed my sheep."*

Through this encounter, Peter is able to embrace his story. Drawing upon the power of Jesus and the mission passed onto Him, He goes out into the world and does remarkable things. Next, we see him preaching so powerfully at Pentecost that the Bible says that three thousand people became followers of Jesus that day! Acts 2:41 reads, *"Those who accepted his message were baptized, and about three thousand were added to their number that day."* That is a HUGE number! Think about the joy and accomplishment we feel when through our ministry, ONE person comes to faith. This is THREE THOUSAND! That is absolutely miraculous. Paul was able to live out his calling in a powerful way without being held back by sin because he had settled his sin.

We, too, have the same potential within us. Just imagine for a moment the incredible things you could do for God's Kingdom.

He has a grand adventure prepared for you. He has planted something within you that He desires to water and watch bloom into something immensely powerful in your life. All you have to do is begin walking a path of faith with Him, all the while seeking out every chance possible to grow in maturity in our faith. This is all possible when we embrace our stories.

We find our voice not in the midst of our trauma, but as a result of overcoming it. When we truly get out from under it to show others that they too can be more than conquerors in Christ, we find our voice. Many people rather chose to live in their trauma, neglecting God and the truth that He is best at taking messy stories and showing His love and truth through them. Allow your soul to rest in the fact that Jesus' truth and love will carry you through anything you ever face so that you can show others that not only can they stand again, but that together we can go on the journey of the life of a settled soul.

Own Your Story

This situation brings to mind Ephesians 2:10, which says, *"For we are his workmanship, created in Christ Jesus for good works, which God prepared beforehand, that we should walk in them."* Keep this verse close to your heart always as you walk in the powerful purpose God has prepared for you.

Own your story and take hold of it. Understand it, know it, and unpack it. Then, ask God to purpose it. When you do this, there is no angst, shame, or desire to run away. You can settle who you are and where you are at. You can embrace all of the intricacies that make you who you are today without feeling the need to hide or run away from anything. You can now share openly, boldly, and confidently. It's that type of witness that's going to be powerful and win hearts for the faith.

I want to tell you the story of two young men, both the same age, who were born only two days apart. They have another thing in common: they both lost their mom in the same year of high school. They both went to the same church, and both believed in the same God. Yet, one used the story of his mom and how much pain and trauma he felt to fuel a fire to become everything he could. He embraced his story for a bigger purpose: to prove to himself that he had something inside of them for the world and the people around them.

The other young man decided to indulge in women and other sins. His soul was unsettled. He embraced a sinful lifestyle instead of fleeing from it. And when things got bad, he pointed his finger at the trauma he experienced in the past. He didn't take ownership of his story and used it to fuel a better life for himself. He let the experiences of his life send him into a spiraling life enslaved by sin.

This story shows us just how important it is that we embrace our story. If we don't, our past will inhibit our future. We will be weighed down by an anchor that will hold us back from achieving everything God has called us to do in this life.

Never forget that God created you in the womb. He made you inside and out: He knows all of your intricacies. Jeremiah 1:5 says, *"Before I formed you in the womb I knew you, before you were born, I set you apart; I appointed you as a prophet to the nations."*

Psalm 139:13-16 says:

"For you created my inmost being; you knit me together in my mother's womb. I praise you because I am fearfully and wonderfully made; your works are wonderful; I know that full well. My frame was not hidden from you when I was made in the secret place when I was woven together in the depths of the earth. Your eyes saw my unformed body; all the days ordained for me were written in your book before one of them came to be."

These verses show clearly how deeply and personally God knows us. He is the one who began our life. He is deeply invested in us. He loves us more than we could ever know. He wants nothing more than to be an integral part of your story. He wants to walk alongside you and help you to write out every detail of it. And who better to welcome along that journey with us than God Himself, the very One who created us?

Individualism and Identity

You are unique and there's nothing wrong with your unique story. There may be messy parts in your story, but your story is what will help make this world a better place. You must choose not to allow what is hurting you to define you but to set the purpose for your unique story. We must take hold of that uniqueness to truly embrace our story so that we can live a life of identity and purpose without falling into the sin of individualism. Knowing our true identity brings about the revelation that our individuality was created by God for the glory of God and that we must do what He has called us to do: love other people. Where our uniqueness comes in is the way in which He has called us to love other people. He has given us unique skills and passions in which to do so.

He's called us to the community, where our story can truly impact the lives of others. It's through our relational nature that our stories are shared (messy parts and all) and where they can impact the hearts of others. We must embrace community and form tight bonds with our fellow believers in Christ.

Our story is the tale of God and the gifts He's given us. Be excited to scale the walls but remember this truth: fulfillment and the embracing of your story ultimately don't come from something you do, but from the many things that God has done and is doing in your life.

We're content, not because our story is completed, but because we're still drawing stickmen. We're still working on the projects that God has placed on our hearts. Allow God's grace to renew and restore you. Then we may actually start over.

Not everyone needs or wants our service. There are seasons when people need help and seasons they don't. All God is asking us to do is to be committed with our unique gifts and unique design for unique situations. We may not feel as though we are walking in our purpose every day, but remember, even though some people may pass you by there will be people that stop because they need what only you can provide. Be ready to provide it for them. That's what we're called to do. Trust that what God's given you is enough. Partner with God in your efforts to settle your story. Then embark on the grand adventure of continuing that story with Him.

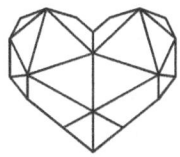

CHAPTER 7
THE CLARITY

"Leave it all in the Hands that were wounded for you."

-Elisabeth Elliot

Diamonds have internal blemishes that you can't see these without the aid of a special magnifying glass. In the same way, there's some stuff inside of us that no one can see. On the outside, we may be looking really good. We may be polished. People may even notice and talk about how well we are doing. But on the inside, we have some undisclosed things going on. We have blemishes. People see the outside, but God sees the inside.

We learn to wear our hurt well. Many of us have figured out how to put on our brave faces and act as if everything is ok. While we have good intentions in doing so, all we are doing is ignoring that pain inside. We must be brave enough to confront our feelings, bring them to the Lord, and seek true healing. God is stronger than anything we are feeling, and He can bring healing to it all. The only requirement is that we trust in Him.

There comes a moment when you have an emotional melt down before the Lord because He sees your inside, He knows the pain, hurt, and anger you are holding on to. Release them to God and be a free woman of God! He will not hold ANYTHING against you!

We must open ourselves up and stop trying to wear the masks of deception, we are not fooling anybody, not even ourselves. We know what's going on in our hearts. We must realize that it's not a sign of weakness to be honest and vulnerable with those Christian sisters that we know we can trust. In fact, it's admirable to seek the help, support, and encouragement you need! It shows a commitment to your all-around health and a desire to walk in the fullness that God has prepared for you.

Don't put off taking action until it's too late. Don't let the strain, pain, and stress of suppressing your emotions build up to the point where you make major life mistakes. Once he sobered up, King Xerxes misses Vashti! He realizes that he has cast aside someone very precious, a blessing in his life. But at this point, it's much too late to reverse what has been done. His story serves as a perfect example of why we must be proactive in processing our feelings and living up to our full potential before we create messes for ourselves when we bottle up what we are feeling inside.

We need to talk about the endurance that grace provides. Grace is foundational to our understanding of our faith. Grace is also an invaluable blessing that allows us to endure the most challenging seasons of our lives. Why is that? Because grace is what fueled Jesus' sacrifice on the cross that brought us all salvation.

Grace looks past our faults and towards the person of extreme worth and value on the inside. With grace, we can look inwards and see that we are so much more than the sinful actions that have been holding us back for so long. We can also grant that same grace to others. In this, there is profound freedom.

2 Corinthians 12:9. God says, *"My grace is all you need. My power works best in weakness."* To fully capture the power of grace, we must realize that we can't do it all on our own. We must push pride to the side, accept our weaknesses, and embrace the presence of the Holy Spirit that lives within us. When we do, the unparalleled power of Christ will flow through us, moving us past a point of desperation into a thriving life where we can finally realize our full potential.

All of this is possible through grace for ourselves and others. Through prayer, ask that God would fill you with the grace that only He can provide. When He does, your heart will be transformed, and your life will change daily from the inside out!

You may think you are something today, but God has called you to be something greater. God knows you better than you even know yourself. He understands exactly what you're capable of and what you can grow into. That's only logical, considering He made you. Psalm 139:13-14 says, *"For you created my inmost being, you knit me together in my mother's womb. I praise you because I am fearfully and wonderfully made; your works are wonderful; I know that full well."*

God made you for a certain purpose that only you can fulfill. He carefully examined your unique perspective, skill set, and personality when putting together His plan for your life. He not only wants you to achieve great things in life, but He also wants you to be fulfilled in the work He has given you.

God wants every area of your life to come together in such a manner that you are complete and at your best. God made you as a work of art, and He desires to bring out every feature that makes you the extremely special and unique person that you are. He understands the impact you can have on the world and wants to guide you in making it happen.

We can do so through relationships, hobbies, education, and a variety of other activities. Unfortunately, it can often feel as if no matter what we invest in or hold to in life, we will never be able to find that tremendous feeling of identity that we crave. The longer we look, the more desperate we get to discover what it is that will define us.

But the truth of the matter is, who we are, rests in Christ alone. God tells us who we are. If our identity rests anywhere else, it is a false identity. We have taken something else and used it to cover our true selves up when our true selves were within us all along. That's because we are defined by the presence of the Holy Spirit within us. That's why we mustn't look towards external influences when trying to grasp who we really are: we must look within towards the things God has specially placed within us.

We may have a twisted perception of ourselves, for good or bad. We don't always see ourselves how we should. But God does. He sees the person and potential within. While we only see a fraction of what's there, God sees the whole picture. The lens through which He sees us isn't distorted like the one through which we see ourselves.

Let's return to the story of the prodigal son, but now let's shift our focus off the prodigal son himself and to the father in the story. No matter what his son has done, he is eager to welcome him home and back into his arms. It doesn't matter that he's wasted the entire inheritance or committed horrendous sins. All the father wants is to see his son come back home. He wants his son to be a part of their family and embrace the true personhood he had left behind. The father recognizes that the son who has gone out into the world is not his true son. The father recognizes that his son has far greater potential. That is why his heart yearns for his son to return home and realize his full potential. That's why he is so overjoyed to see his son returning home! His joy is so great that he brushes aside the sins his son committed against him. All of that doesn't matter anymore. He wants to give everything he can to his son so that he can become everything that is inside of him. He pushes away any feelings of hurt or anger because he wants to encourage his son along his reformed path. He doesn't want to discourage his son by coming down hard on him.

There's a deeper truth behind this story. This story is a direct parallel to how God looks at us! We have strayed far from him, taking with us the blessings He had endowed us with. We squander them in pursuit of a life contrary to our faith and the guidance of the Holy Spirit within us. Instead of following God, we follow our own selfish desires and sinful urges.

The problem is that being enslaved to sin is part of our human nature since Adam and Eve's transgression in the Garden of Eden. Paul talks about it in such a relatable way in Romans 7:14-17: "*So the trouble is not with the law, for it is spiritual and good. The trouble is with me, for I am all too human, a slave to sin. I don't really understand myself, for I want to do what is right, but I don't do it. Instead, I do what I hate. But if I know that what I am doing is wrong, this shows that I agree that the law is good. So, I am not the one doing wrong; it is sin living in me that does it."*

How often do we feel like this? We have a desire to do good, but we do wrong anyway. That's because we are fighting the sinful nature within us. Our enemy is not flesh and blood, but the spiritual forces of sin that Satan uses against us. It is impossible for us to fight against, and that's exactly why Jesus came to save us. Through Him, we have the freedom to ascend past our sinful nature.

There must come to a point, like with the prodigal son, when we realize that this way of life, we've strayed so far in order to embrace is actually holding us back from our true potential. God's love and power are so close, yet we run in the other direction. But through the sacrifice of Jesus, God overlooks our grave error and welcomes us back home into His loving arms. He rejoices for every lost person who turns back towards Him. His love for us is everlasting and unconditional.

There, by the side of our heavenly Father, we rediscover our true selves. God pulls away from the blinders over our eyes and we see a genuine look at ourselves again. There are no more worldly influences to skew our perception of ourselves. God shows us exactly who He created us to be. This is a life-altering opportunity that God gives us. When we have this moment with God, we will never be the same.

Even when tough times come, we can still rest assured that God's plans are firmly in place. Romans 8:28-30 says, *"And we know that in all things God works for the good of those who love him, who have been called according to his purpose. For those God foreknew he also predestined to be conformed to the image of his Son, that he might be the firstborn among many brothers and sisters. And those he predestined, he also called; those he called, he also justified; those he justified, he also glorified."*

God can take any circumstance in your life and use it for good. Whether it's a trial that builds character, a tragedy that can become a testimony, or a setback that can help you come back stronger, God can use it for good. Never doubt or limit His power, even when it seems as if the world is working against you. God is mightier than anything you face.

God chose you for greatness. He wants to make you more like Jesus. He has called you out of your former life into new life. That new life is a life of power and purpose. He has justified you through the blood of Jesus Christ, and as His child, you share in His glory. Let His image shine radiantly through all you do.

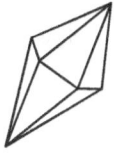

CHAPTER 8
THE PRESSURE

"Never give up, for that is just the place and time that the tide will turn."

-Harriet Beecher Stowe

Diamonds can only form under extremely high pressure. There is no other way to make them! God has given us everything we need to not succumb to the pressures of this world but to overcome them by the power of our testimony. There is no shame in what you have been through without the pressure the struggles and the pain you would not have the wisdom understanding and growth you have today.

We do not begin our lives walking in our full potential. The demands and experiences of life, together with a vibrant relationship with God mold us into the individuals we were designed to be. This implies that we must alter our outlook on the challenges we confront in life. We must neither regard them negatively nor lament their presence. We must instead embrace them!

As you experience these pressures in your life, turn them over to God in prayer and ask Him to use them as opportunities to help you grow in every way. See every experience, good or bad, as a chance to learn. Everything in life can teach us a lesson and help us to grow on our path of spiritual maturity. God wants to use your experiences to guide you to your fullest potential in Him.

Remember that God will never give you more than you can handle. 1 Corinthians 10:13 says, *"No temptation has overtaken you except what is common to mankind. And God is faithful; he will not let you be tempted beyond what you can bear. But when you are tempted, he will also provide a way out so that you can endure it."*

God will equip you with everything you need to overcome anything that comes your way in life. All you have to do is walk with Him and invest richly in your relationship with Him.

We are going to look at some stories of prominent women from the Bible who took the pressures in their life and turned them into opportunities to make an impact on the story of God's people.

Hagar (Gen. 16:1–16; 21:8–21)

Hagar's story is full of God's goodness. Her story is a prime example of how God works in our lives, even in the most unlikely of circumstances. Hagar's story starts off where in society's eyes, she is a nobody. She is simply a slave girl with no social status or influence. Many would look down upon her and treat her as insignificant. Not only that, but she didn't even have faith to rely on because she didn't know the God of Abraham.

Hagar was Abraham's slave girl. When Sarah couldn't bear children for Abraham, she gave Hagar to him to bear his child instead. When Hagar became pregnant with Ishmael, Sarah became fiercely jealous and made Abraham cast Hagar and her son out. She and Ishmael found themselves wandering in the desert with limited supplies.

Eventually, their food and water ran out. With her hope quickly fading, Hagar placed Ismael under a bush and walked away so that she wouldn't have to witness his death. As she wept, the Lord reached out to her in her distress. God led her to a well of water that saved her and Ishmael's life.

Hagar is such a profound influence and example for us because even in the direst of circumstances, she was able to recognize the presence of God. He reached out for her, and she responded to His presence with faith. How do you respond to circumstances outside of your control? Do you recognize God's presence alongside you and gracefully accept His provisions? Or do you try to wrestle control of the situation yourself? We would do well to emulate the faith of Hagar as we come up against the pressures of life.

Rebekah (Genesis 27-29)

We can learn a lot from Rebekah, both good and bad. As we will see in her story, she was very much human. She was a woman with a good heart who was inspired by Isaac's devout faith, but she fell victim to sin and deception, as we all do. But nonetheless, God was still faithful in her life. This is also true of us. None of us are without sin, but God still loves us, guides us, and is always by our side despite our shortcomings.

Rebekah was faithful to the Lord's calling in marrying Isaac and raising a family by his side. She followed Abraham's servant faithfully and trusted in the Lord. It wasn't until she had twin sons, Jacob, and Esau, that she ran across sin in her life.

Esau was to receive his father's blessing, as he was the eldest son. But Rebekah favored Jacob and devised a plan to deceive Isaac into giving his blessing to Jacob instead. Her plan worked, with Jacob receiving their father's blessing. But the deception was quickly exposed, and Jacob had to run for his life to avoid the vengeance from Esau. This sad and troubling family situation was brought about by Rebekah's sin.

God's goodness and constancy were evident in Rebekah's life. God's providence led to Rebekah's marriage to Isaac, her pregnancy was a response to prayer, and her boys' lives fulfilled prophesy. Rebekah's decision to lie and deceive her husband exemplifies how human wrongdoing does not block God's plans and how, despite our wickedness, God may ultimately bring about His will via His kindness and wisdom. When we reflect upon our own lives, it's helpful to look at them through a similar lens. If we look closely, we will see God at work throughout our lives despite our circumstances, just as He did with Rebekah.

Even when we slip up, God can use those circumstances for good while at the same time teaching us a powerful lesson on how to better handle the pressures before us in the future!

Jochebed (Exodus 1-2)

Jochebed was the daughter of Levi, the third of Jacob's sons. She was born just as Jacob and his family entered Egypt, where they were destined to be cruelly enslaved. She married Amram and became the mother of Moses, Aaron, and Miriam.

When the Jewish people were enslaved in Egypt, Pharaoh ordered that all newborn Jewish baby boys be put to death. See what happened according to Exodus 1: 15-17: *"The king of Egypt said to the Hebrew midwives, whose names were Shiphrah and Puah, when you are helping the Hebrew women during childbirth on the delivery stool, if you see that the baby is a boy, kill him; but if it is a girl, let her live." The midwives, however, feared God and did not do what the king of Egypt had told them to do; they let the boys live."*

Jochebed defied Pharoah and raised her son until she couldn't hide him anymore. She put him in a basket (Exodus 2) which she then put in the River Nile. Thankfully, Pharoah's daughter found her son, Moses and he was saved. From Jochebed's story, we learn that it's not enough to know what's right and wrong— we must have the strength to carry out our convictions. She did what she knew was right, even at the risk of her life, and God protected and rewarded her. She did what she knew was right, despite the immense pressures facing her and in the end; God was glorified.

Deborah (Judges 4)

Deborah was a judge and ruler of Israel. She led Israel against the Canaanites, their King Jabin, and their military general Sisera, calling on a Jewish warrior named Barak to command Israel's army.

To Deborah's request, Barak famously replied, *"If you will go with me, then I will go; but if you will not go with me, I will not go"* (Judges 4:8). Deborah would agree to accompany Barak. However, she informed him that, because of his hesitancy, *"The honor shall not be yours… for the Lord will sell Sisera into the hands of a woman"* (Judges 4:9).

Deborah's prophecy would soon come to fruition.

As Israel routed Sisera's forces at Mount Tabor, Sisera, the Canaanite general, escaped, seeking refuge in the tent of Jael, the wife of Heber the Kenite (Judges 4:17). But as Canaan's top military leader slept soundly, Jael shoved a tent spike through Sisera's head, killing him where he lay (Judges 4:21). With his army decimated and trusted general now watering the sand with a spike-shaped hole in his head, Jabin, the king of Canaan, was soon defeated. The people of Israel were liberated from the Canaanites (Judges 7:24). Deborah and Barak would then sing of this victory, praising God for His faithfulness and deliverance of their people. One of the first examples of Hebrew poetry recorded in the Bible is the Song of Deborah and Barak (Judges 5).

Deborah's leadership over God's people in such a male-dominated society in and of itself is inspiring. But she took it a step further. She was a wise, strong, and influential leader on top of it. She led God's people to victory and was a compassionate judge over them all. In any leadership opportunities we face, we would be wise to emulate Deborah's influence.

Can you imagine the crazy amount of pressure she faced as the leader of the Israelites? She was accountable before her people and before God. She had to lead the people in every way: Socially, religiously, and in war. But Deborah leaned upon her strength in the Lord and gives us a remarkable example to follow in our own lives.

These remarkable women's stories are prime instances of how pressure can shape, mold, and complete our identities and power. They were all put through various trials and hardships. But, through it all, God was faithful and blessed them with godly fruit that has influenced many people to this day.

Commit to shifting your perspective on how you view the pressures in your life. Remember, pressure makes diamonds. In the same way, pressure will shape you, mold you, and bring your ultimate potential to fruition.

CHAPTER 9
THE RESOLUTION

"The Christian life is not about all the things we do for God--it's about being loved by Him, loving Him in return, and walking in intimate union and communion with Him."

-Nancy Leigh DeMoss

We must live our life to the utmost and be ALL that God has made us to be now that we understand how wonderful we are. We must be willing to walk away from all the things in life that have hampered us, just as Vashti did. Vashti walked away from the throne, the castle, and all the material possessions that came with it, but she kept her dignity.

Let's discuss about Rahab's story for a bit. It all started when Joshua sent spies to Jericho to see what he and the Israelites were up against after the Lord told them to capture the land.

Rahab saved the spies at great danger to herself. In Joshua 2:9-11, Rahab says, "*I know that the LORD has given you this land*

and that a great fear of you has fallen on us, so that all who live in this country are melting in fear because of you. We have heard how the LORD dried up the water of the Red Sea for you when you came out of Egypt, and what you did to Sihon and Og, the two kings of the Amorites east of the Jordan, whom you completely destroyed. When we heard of it, our hearts melted in fear and everyone's courage failed because of you, for the LORD your God is God in heaven above and on the earth below."

Rahab proclaims her belief in God. Rahab had enough sense to realize that these were men of God. She understood that their God can do powerful things. She said, "I believe in your God."

Joshua 2:12-14 reads, *"Now then, please swear to me by the LORD that you will show kindness to my family, because I have shown kindness to you. Give me a sure sign that you will spare the lives of my father and mother, my brothers, and sisters, and all who belong to them—and that you will save us from death." "Our lives for your lives!" the men assured her. "If you don't tell what we are doing, we will treat you kindly and faithfully when the LORD gives us the land."*

Rahab trusted in the Lord's might and knew He could save her family when no one else could. She took a bold step forward in faith and asked that Joshua would save her family's life because she had favored them. Generational blessings are waiting on your deeds. Woman of God, do good at the slightest opportunity you have. Lot entertained Angels and his kindness saved him and his family from the destruction of Sodom and Gomorrah (Genesis 19).

There are people connected to you that are waiting on you for your obedience. People are looking forward to your acts because

God has called you to break your family's generational curses. God has so much more in store for you, as well as your family! Because of the blood of Jesus, you can become everything God has called you to be! Because of the blood, no matter what curses your family faces, things can change! There is redemption through the blood of Jesus.

In Joshua 2:15, Rahab helps the spies escape the city with a cord that she drops down from her window. When you study the word cord, the Hebrew word for cord is shovel: it means pain, sorrow, travail. So many times, in life, we keep that cord close to us. We carry our hurt, we carry our pain, and we carry our sorrows. It becomes the tool we use.

In Joshua 2:16-18 says, *"She said to them, "Go to the hills so the pursuers will not find you. Hide yourselves there three days until they return, and then go on your way." Now the men had said to her, "This oath you made us swear will not be binding on us unless, when we enter the land, you have tied this scarlet cord in the window through which you let us down, and unless you have brought your father and mother, your brothers and all your family into your house."*

Because of Rahab's actions and her belief in God, she received redemption. Beloved, God has prepared you, unlock your potentials and reach out to as many souls as you can. You may be a Rahab to someone out there. You may help someone take away their burden, fear, anguish, hate and deliver them into God's marvelous light. What are you going to do with your time? God has given you brand new grace and brand-new mercies. The time is now to accomplish what God has given you to do.

God desires for all of us to be both leaders and influencers. In the failure of leadership, there is a failure of the heart. It's essential that we do the work necessary to get our hearts right.

Confidence and Courage

The Lord spoke to Joshua. He told him, "Moses is dead, it's your time." He gave us all a charge to take courage, just as He did for Joshua. He desires that we'd take a hold of our dreams, for now, is our time! But so many of us continue to harbor the spirit of Moses, thinking we are unqualified and unprepared. How can it be my time? Have you ever asked yourself that?

Moses had a speech impediment, but the Lord asks Him to speak on behalf of the people. Moses was afraid to speak before Pharoah, he had many questions that reflected his doubt. He asked, *"Who should I tell them sent me?"* and God's response to him was, *"I am that I am!"*

You don't deserve the position

You are unqualified

You are never going to make it…

Do not for one moment doubt yourself! Do not for one moment allow others project their fears into your life! YOU ARE THE DAUGHTER OF "I AM!" When people say what they believe, respond along this line, "I've heard you, but I Am has sent me!"

Moses talked to God face to face like a friend. There's a difference in how you handle your response when there's a relationship. Even beyond his shortcomings, he was able to go forward because he was confident in his relationship with the Lord. He knew the almighty power of God at work within him.

There is real power in a relationship. Dialogue develops a relationship.

The devil breeds so much negativity within our hearts. But all we need to combat it is to know God's deep and everlasting love for us. We need to embrace His power in our lives and know that His promises are true. We must eagerly anticipate the things He has prepared for us.

Jeremiah 29:11-14 says, *"For I know the plans I have for you,"* declares the LORD, *"plans to prosper you and not to harm you, plans to give you hope and a future. Then you will call on me and come and pray to me, and I will listen to you. You will seek me and find me when you seek me with all your heart. I will be found by you,"* declares the LORD, *"and will bring you back from captivity. I will gather you from all the nations and places where I have banished you,"* declares the LORD, *"and will bring you back to the place from which I carried you into exile."*

So many times, we think we're just talking through prayer, but we must know that through our relationship with God, we not only pray, but God responds!

What you are in need of has already been released. The power of Jesus can break every chain. I am releasing you from the captivity of the pain you've experienced. What people have said or done to you, etc. I will return everything that has been taken from you.

The difference-maker is when our vision becomes our glory. You must see yourself through the heart of God. Turn your blurry vision into bloody vision. There's nothing you need that the blood of Christ hasn't made compensation for. There's nothing you will ever come against that the blood of Christ has not already defeated. The blood is mentioned 427 times in the Bible, from the first book to the very last book. Everything in our relationship with God is hinged upon the blood. Oftentimes we speak of the blood, but I think we still underestimate the full power of the blood.

I Am means that whatever you need, God is! Whatever you need, the blood of Christ is. Leviticus 17:11 reads, *"For the life of a creature is in the blood, and I have given it to you to make atonement for yourselves on the altar; it is the blood that makes atonement for one's life."* The blood makes atonement for you! The blood is life! Our natural blood carries oxygen throughout our body. It causes all the organs in our body to function properly. When you look at the spiritual blood, it's the blood that gives us life!

The blood says, "I am peace." Colossians 1:19-20 says, *"For God was pleased to have all his fullness dwell in him, and through him to reconcile to himself all things, whether things on earth or things in heaven, by making peace through his blood, shed on the cross."* All the negative things the enemy has spoken into your mind are nothing compared to the peace God pours into your heart. God says He will give you peace that will surpass your understanding. It will guard your heart and mind!

Somebody will always come to try and steal your peace. People will always try to say something against you, why you aren't called, why you aren't qualified, but the blood of Christ brings the peace you need to overcome all the negativity and turn it into power!

Say it with me, woman of God, ***"I am everything God has called me to be!"***

The blood says, "I am justification." Romans 5:8-11 reads:

"But God demonstrates his own love for us in this: While we were still sinners, Christ died for us. Since we have now been justified by his blood, how much more shall we be saved from God's wrath through him! For if, while we were God's enemies, we were reconciled to him through the death of his Son, how much more, having been reconciled, shall we be saved through his life! Not only is this so, but we also boast in God through our Lord Jesus Christ, through whom we have now received reconciliation."

Tell your problems, circumstances, and situations, "I have been justified!" Christ died for us because we couldn't be perfect all our life. We have been made righteous by His blood. No matter what you see in the mirror, God has made you righteous. It's time to see yourself righteous, justified, whole, and free.

Because of the blood, we have joy in God. We don't have joy in the condition of this world. We don't have joy predicated on who likes us or doesn't like us. We don't have joy because the world gave it to me. We have joy because we have the blood of Jesus! God's justification brings me joy.

The blood says, "I am the cleanser." 1 John 1:7-10 reads, *"But if we walk in the light, as he is in the light, we have fellowship with one another, and the blood of Jesus, his Son, purifies us from all sin. If we claim to be without sin, we deceive ourselves and the truth is not in us. If we confess our sins, he is faithful and just and will forgive us our sins and purify us from all unrighteousness. If we claim we have not sinned, we make him out to be a liar and his word is not in us."*

God has already cleaned our messes up! The best day of my life was the day I realized I am a sinner. It made me know that I needed the blood of Jesus!

The blood says, "I am redemption" (Ephesians 4:7-9). Grace means I didn't get what I deserved. Rather, God has blessed me abundantly despite the factor that I haven't earned it or deserved it. God's redemption, love, and blessings come from an overflow of His great love and not from anything I have done. It's all about God and what He has done for me.

The blood says, "I am righteousness" (Romans 3:23-26). There's nothing you can do to earn His grace. Instead, He has chosen to give it freely. Through the blood, we are clothed with the righteousness of Christ. When we stand before the Lord, He no longer sees us and our sin, but He rather sees Christ and the righteousness He has earned on our behalf.

Rest in the salvation that God has freely given you through the blood of Christ! When you take hold of this miraculous gift, you will be able to shine brilliantly just like the diamond you are!

CONCLUSION

"Unless we form the habit of going to the Bible in bright moments as well as in trouble, we cannot fully respond to its consolations because we lack equilibrium between light and darkness."

-Helen Keller

Your words have great power to influence your life. You can make declarations about your purpose and identity that can change your life in ways you could never imagine before. The things we declare will manifest themselves in one of two ways: either to our prosperity or to our failure. Proverbs 18:21 says, *"The tongue has the power of life and death, and those who love it will eat its fruit."* If we declare good and godly things that are aligned with His will for our life, we will see to fruition the fulfillment of our ultimate potential in Him. If we declare worldly and selfish things in our lives, we will reap the harvest of those as well.

In Matthew 6:21, Jesus says, *"For where your treasure is, there your heart will be also."* What Jesus is teaching us here is that what we choose to invest our time and energy in will have a huge impact on our lives.

It has both positive and negative consequences. For example, if you spend your time and energy to worldly pursuits such as wealth building while putting your faith on the back burner, you'll begin to live a life apart from the abundant life that comes with faith in Christ. However, if you make Bible reading, prayer, and fellowship a priority in your life, your connection with God will blossom! To borrow a well-known expression, ***"you will reap what you sow!"*** That is why sowing seeds of righteousness and faith in our life is critical.

Your mind must be renewed daily because where your mind is your head will follow. Out of the abundance of the heart, the mouth will speak. What's on the inside will come out. If the word of God is in your heart it will flow out of your mouth. If your heart is filled with negativity, hatred, jealousy, etc., it likewise will come out. Word curses are real! If you say you're broke, you will be broken. The word of God says He has never seen the righteous forsaken nor His seed begging for bread. He showers favors on us on a regular basis, and He has given us the ability to obtain wealth! I will not go hungry since the Lord is my Shepherd!

Many today believe that the Bible is merely an old and outdated book with nothing to offer the modern world. This could not be more false! Every new generation of believers will find plenty of wisdom in the Bible! This current perception is essentially an illusion of the enemy. In fact, the world now more than ever requires God's Word!

Within its pages, the Bible reveals the truth about God, about us, and the world we live in. God breathes love, identity, and purpose into our lives via it. We grow in our connection with

God when we spend time in His Word every day. He shares His power with us through that relationship. The Bible is the key to completely accepting and walking in our role as God's children!

He has called us to be a light to a world of darkness and a messenger of His Word. The Words we speak into the world have a lasting impact that we could never even know. That's precisely why God has equipped us with His Holy Spirit and called us to spread the Good News of the Gospel all over the earth. We must declare His love and truth not only in our own lives but to the people we encounter daily.

God has put this profound calling on our lives and He fills us with everything we need to see it through to fruition. God has created you as a unique individual with something special to offer the world, all for the glory and building up of His eternal Kingdom. He places dreams within our hearts so that we can walk in the purpose He has prepared and equipped us for.

Why are we afraid to pursue our dreams when God has not given us a spirit of fear? You must speak this word over your life daily! He tells us several times in the Bible to be not afraid! But are we really listening to Him?

Your breakthrough is coming!

Honor your father and mother. We have so many issues and struggles in our world today because we don't know how to honor and value others.

It's hard to honor God as our Abba because we tried to put God in our earthly place. We think about the father relationships we've had in our lives. For many of us, the sad reality is that our fathers were absent or not a very real presence in our lives. We then, wrongly attribute those experiences to God Himself. We put in him the box with our earthly father. We're in the world, but we're not of the world. The same is true with God!

We have to take God out of that box and understand that He is greater than whatever circumstances you have faced or are currently facing. We're afraid God won't be there for us just like our earthly father wasn't.

Nothing you will come up against is too hard for God to overcome Abba Father. There is no need you will experience that He cannot fulfill. There is no trial you will come up against that is mightier than His almighty power.

God has created some amazing women. He has anointed you; He has appointed you, and He has gifted you. But you don't see your self-worth. It's hard to find your self-worth because you don't see the value within yourself.

When God created you, He was intentional. Before you were in your mother's womb, He knew you! He knew your mother and father; He knew the family you would be born into. Just as Jesus was foretold to come through the line of David.

Your life has been predestined. All the gifts God has placed within you are for a purpose. God doesn't make mistakes. He knows precisely what He was doing when He created you, for He had envisioned you beforehand!

There are things in your heritage that will come through your family line that will be important to your story. God knows that, and He was intentional.

God has dressed you fully in your purpose. You have a unique calling and gifting based on God's plan and purpose for your life.

There is a distinction between what you can do and what God has called you to do. You can do certain things on your own, but when God has called you to something greater, you can't achieve it until you let Him do it through you! If God has called you to it, He will assist you in seeing it through. No matter how magnificent the calling may appear, don't limit the Lord's power in your life.

You must allow the Lord and His power to enter your life.

You must know how to move when God speaks. So frequently, we have the blinders on and miss God's voice, and we don't move in the way we're supposed to. This way, we miss out on so many amazing possibilities in life! When we think back to the man who had been paralyzed for 28 years at Bethesda's pool. "Do you want to be healed?" Jesus asks plaintively. To be healed, all the man had to do was say "yes!" and receive Christ.

So often, God speaks into our lives with simple questions like this and all we have to say is "yes!" so that you may receive His blessings.

Let your "yes" guide you to your fullest potential in Christ. Woman of God, become the diamond that God has destined for you to be. Shine brilliantly and make an impact on this world the way that only you can!

Wisdom Speaks

I had a lunch date with three of my close friends. They were 92-, 86-, and 82-years young at the time. Once we were settled in at the restaurant, I explained to them that I was writing a book to women to encourage them in understanding just how valuable they are to God and asked them if they could share a few words of encouragement to a woman today, what would they say to her, and what they shared was very heartfelt wisdom worth passing on.

The 92-year-old shared she would tell her "She is Enough". She went on to explained that she lived most of her life trying to live up to the expectations of others that she lost herself in the process. She shared things only changed when the accepted that she was fearfully and wonderfully made just as God created her; and that "She Was Enough".

The 86-year-old shared she would tell her "She is Beautiful". She said it breaks her heart to see so many young women who don't realize just how beautiful they are as God has made everything beautiful in his time; she knows that "She is Beautiful".

The baby of the bunch, the 82-year-old said she would tell her to "Learn to Listen". She shared that there were so many mistakes she made in life all because she refused to accept wisdom from others; the learned the way of a fool is right is his own eyes, but a wise person listens to advise. "She Learned to Listen".

I was blessed to have been in the presence of almost 300 years of living wisdom seated at one table. I am just as grateful to have the opportunity to share it with you.

Woman of God, learn to accept wisdom. You are Enough. You are Beautiful. You are Valuable!! Live in your purpose!!

www.ingramcontent.com/pod-product-compliance
Lightning Source LLC
Chambersburg PA
CBHW031636160426
43196CB00006B/438